D1286633

The Life and Times
of a Country Jurist

Stephen L. Boyles

McFadden Books
Orlando

McFadden Books ~ An imprint of Waterview Press, Inc.

February 2003.
Cover design by John Hodge
Back cover photo of Judge Boyles by Tom Deputy
Edited by Jim Mast
Distributed by Mickler's Books, Inc., Oviedo, Fla. 32765
          www.micklers.com

Library of Congress Catologuing-in-Publication Data
Boyles, Stephen L., 12/30/1934 --
Details will be furnished upon request.

ISBN 1-883114-15-2

Dedication

These memoirs are dedicated to:

The memory of Lloyd and Corinne, Pa (Leslie Pigue), Miss Florence, Lieutenant Colonel Oscar Emery,Jr. Miss Kate (Kate Walton Engelklen) and Brigadier General William M.. Thames,Jr.

Miss Sara, a true class act as daughter, mother, grand-mother, wife and human being.

My children, Leslie, Stephen Jr., Allyson, and Dell; and our grandchildren, Brandy, Stephen, Lauren, Brandon, Lloyd, Sean, Ryan, Christopher, Cody and Savannah; my sister Nelline and all members of our extended families; and my "family of friends."

The NCOIC at Ernest Harmon Air Force Base who jump started my professional career.

My team of loyal and dedicated workers in the Office of the State Attorney. They were one helluva group and some now describe my 20-year tenure as "the days of Camelot."

To my judicial law clerks, Pamela, Chris, Marilyn and April. They were forever enhancing the products of my talents and only now can they claim some credit.

Acknowledgments

The evolving of my genealogy (for the children) into memoirs, then to manuscript and finally to publication was an endeavor, like most of my endeavors, which did not occur without substantial help.

Ralph Willis, a newcomer close friend and fishing partner had the onus of having to listen to this tale repeatedly; he had to listen to the fretting over retirement ad nauseam. Without his encouragement and feedback it is doubtful that I would have sustained the commitment.

Susan Raymond, my typist, was akin to Ralph as a "consultant" but she also put together several runs for little pay and would accept none for the last run.

Miss Sara was the ultimate consultant concerning grammar, content and style. Without her it could not have happened because our shared memories were necessary for accuracy.

Without my children's encouragement it likely would have floundered.

Jim Mast, co author of Bloody Sunset in St. Augustine, and a cracker boy like me, became my editor, pro bono. We, at least from my view, became pallbearer close. Without Jim's wisdom, professional knowledge and encouragement it would only be a manuscript for the children and descendants. When I expressed deep concern for my privacy (if it was published) he simply but poignantly stated "It's a tale that ought to be told."

Contents

Introduction

This is a true tale about my life and times. I reluctantly put it to paper because by nature I am shy, if not bashful, and this can't be done without a little tooting of my horn. Additionally, I have almost arrived at a stage in life where most people simply do what they want to do and prattle repetitiously about what they've done or accomplished. The tale was originally written as a memoir only for the benefit of my children. They and my wife then suggested that it be put into manuscript form. The manuscript contains minor modification of the memoirs. A good example of this is the omission of a rather lengthy genealogy in chapter one. They believe that it may be worthy of print, but if not, very valuable to the grandchildren and their descendants in understanding that who they are is partly a product of where they came from. I found no rebuttal to that position because it continues to be a revelation to me as will fully appear in this text.

The title *Country Jurist* is self-imposed and I am confident about "country" being accurate. Whether I am justified in adding "jurist" will be for the reader to judge. *Webster* defines jurist as "one skilled in the law, especially an eminent judge, lawyer or legal scholar." I personally believe that one cannot attain that status without a richly experienced personal life and my wealth of family and friends would seem to qualify as that foundation.

This manuscript is about a country boy who, early on, believed that he would abide by his roots and inclination and be a rural farmer, but as an Air Force Assistant Staff Judge

Advocate, Staff Judge Advocate; Florida Assistant State Attorney, State Attorney and Circuit Judge wound up exercising jurisdiction over the life, liberty and property of thousands of his fellow men and women. It highlights the most difficult and apparently newsworthy cases. Some of the cases you may recognize from national and international publicity.

Mentally cataloging the subject matter, in order to organize the writing, I became acutely aware that it has been a long road. As an aside I note my amazement that it didn't take more time to travel.

So that you will know who I am, I will begin by telling you from where I came.

1

Citra and Island Grove — the early years

My twin sister Nelline and I were born in Citra, Florida during the afternoon of December 30, 1934. Present at our birth were our maternal Grandmother Nellie Rickenbaker and two pre-teenage aunts (Myrtice and Christine Rickenbaker). Dr. Strange from McIntosh arrived before my sister's birth. Like our father, we grew up to be dark-haired with blue eyes and olive complexion doubtless due to our Black Irish ancestry. As a child, I was a towhead.

Both the Boyles and Rickenbaker families, as Americans, originated in rural low country South Carolina. They tended to be farmers, cattlemen and timber/cotton producer/haulers. Those who migrated to Florida tended to be the same, except for cotton. We twins were born of the marriage of Stephen Lloyd Boyles and Martha Corinne Rickenbaker. Lloyd's father was Stephen Hamilton Boyles and his great-great grandfather settled in Sparr, Florida (about five miles south of Citra) during the early 1830s.

Lloyd and Corinne were hardworking, God-fearing, caring and loving parents. Neither was a regular churchgoer but they regularly tithed and I believe literally lived by the Ten Commandments. They did insist that we twins regularly attend church and for my part that included a heavily starched white shirt, tie, coat, pants and black and white saddle oxfords. It goes without saying that they expected us to live by the same commandments. Early on I discovered that most of the time we did things Mama's way and if the twins did not do it her way there were sanctions. Mama admitted to no grey areas on issues of right and wrong. Our parents were both strong, kind and gentle, but Mama suffered misbehavior poorly, and early on for the most part we toed the line.

By the time Nelline and I were about seven years old our parents' industry paid off. They purchased for cash a home with electricity, running water, space heater and gas stove. They also purchased a grocery store which included a small suite of living quarters. The house and store were located in the hamlet of Island Grove, Florida. Island Grove was two miles north of Citra. The store was on US 301 and about 200 yards east of our home and about the same distance west of a two-room school house. The store premises included a Shell Oil gravity dispensing gas pump. This pump had a ten-gallon clear cylinder atop the pump and by a hand pump, gasoline was pumped up into the cylinder which visibly revealed the volume. Gravity forced the gasoline through a hose for delivery.

At that pump dispensing gas to tourists, I learned that Northerners were different. The women wore sandals over socks and the men never wore striped railroad overalls. They all spoke rapidly with a strange version of English and were always in a hurry. I later learned they did not eat frog legs or grits.

The remainder of business and government in downtown Island Grove included only another small store, Ms. Cason's citrus fruit stand, a citrus packing plant, a depot and a one-room post office. We were not blessed with heavy traffic, concrete, crime or skyscrapers. Ferris Bryant, an Ocala lawyer (later to become Governor) came to our store to prepare our tax returns. For his service we fed him lunch and gave him sacks of farm produce much fresher than he could buy in Ocala. Law and order in the town were provided by Noel Moore, a part-time deputy sheriff, but that was more than sufficient because there was almost no crime and very little in the way of disputes. These were not hustle-bustle times.

Daddy earned $100 per week as a road construction superintendent and the store netted an average of $150 per week. He earned additional money by harvesting and selling alligator hides and frog legs. I often accompanied him in that endeavor. Our food was, of course, wholesale to us. I earned one cent on the dollar on all groceries, gas and farm feed which I handled. Having my own pocket money was important, but more importantly I learned that earned money was more precious than windfall. My mother, without saying a word, taught me frugality.

Island Grove is in southeast Alachua county, about ten miles south of Hawthorne, about four miles east of Cross Creek and about two miles north of Citra. *Cross Creek* was the subject of one book written by Marjorie Kinnon Rawlings. *The Yearling*, another of her books, impeccably described the general topography surrounding these small hamlets. Had Ms. Rawlings, a store customer and good friend of my mother, waited a few years she could have written a real life story of a country boy savoring the woods and lakes of the area. The Yearling did depict "Boyles store" as an establishment often visited by Jody and his family.

When I was between seven and twelve years of age I, with friends, pursued frogs, catfish and bream in the local lakes. We hunted quail, dove and wild turkey and found out in the process that quail were easier to trap than to shoot. "Grunting" worms in the wet flatlands adjacent to Orange

Lake would produce a two-pound coffee can of fish bait in about two minutes. "Grunting" was simply driving a four-foot 1" by 4" board about two feet in the ground and then sliding a brick across the top of the board to create an underground vibration. The vibrations, for reasons unknown to us, caused the worms to surface and crawl across the soil. The fresh game and fish were welcome additions to our diet.

During the summer of 1943 some friends and I were returning from fishing on a blistering July afternoon. We were hot, tired, sweaty and thirsty, and our return home led us through Noel Moore's watermelon field. Temptation prevailed, and we opened and ate a melon without severing it from the vine. Mr. Moore was watching and when we saw him we ran.

When I arrived home I saw Mr. Moore's car backing out of the yard. For my violation of the eighth (Don't steal) Commandment, judgment and sentencing were only moments away. Punishment was swift and painful. It was an old fashioned "whupping" but not a beating. There is a big difference in the two. It was little comfort to learn later in law school that under common law only personal property can be the subject of larceny and an un-severed watermelon was real property. Thus my true crime was only trespass. Nevertheless the crime, its verdict, judgment and sentence occurred in less than an hour. It worked. I had been forever deterred from coveting my neighbor's property.

That night I had to memorize the Ten Commandments and listen in detail about how we would feel if groceries were unlawfully removed from our store. Much later I was told that my mother had referred to her twins as "perfect children" and I interpreted that as having been forgiven for the melon episode. My burden was lighter.

My quality of life and its direction were enhanced by frequent visits to the Rickenbaker grandparents. Miss Nellie, my grandmother, was one of my fishing partners and she was inclined to cook special treats for us twins. She was a regular church goer and had ready biblical references to support her assessment of whether our behavior was proper or improper. These lessons often occurred as we roamed the woods looking for blueberries, blackberries and swamp cabbage. She taught me how to milk a cow and my sister how to make fresh butter. The smell of her kitchen was a delight in itself and partly so because she cooked on a wood stove.

On hog killing day, which came with the first frost, she rendered lard in a large cast iron pot fired by a hardwood fire. A by-product of the lard was miniature chunks of delicious fat meat called "cracklins." They were half-inch squares of the skin still attached to the layer of fat. Part of the lard was later used to make lye soap.

Grandfather, Jeater Lewis Rickenbaker, was a man of few words, many skills and much love. I suspect that he was warned by Mother that she would not tolerate a spoiled son. He was my mentor in carpentry, citrus tree care, farming and cattle raising. I still raise my own citrus and I keep a small herd of cows. Cow care I approached as serious work, keeping to myself the enjoyment it created. Cow care included saddling my pony and loading her, along with Grandfather's grey mare, into a small antiquated International pickup truck.

I don't know how old Grandfather was when he learned to drive but I did notice that he drove the truck as if it was being pulled by a mule that would not leave the road nor run into a tree. We often went to the woods, located the herd and inspected the cows for health and pregnancy. He would rope those needing medical care and all had to be herded through a narrow in-ground dipping vat which included a proper

amount of insecticide. Screw worms were then very preva-
lent and had to be medically treated. Screw worms embedded
themselves in wounds and lived off the infected flesh.

That done, we were usually rewarded with home-grown
home-cured country ham, Carolina style. Homemade cathead
biscuits, fresh eggs from the yard and cheese grits rounded
out the feast. Fresh blueberry pie was the in-season dessert
of choice.

As I grew older I recalled Grandmother's detailed description of their move from South Carolina to Forsyth, Georgia.
The move was made in a mule and wagon, took several weeks,
and they were always given free food and lodging in private
homes. Grandmother was the sister of "Jeat's" first wife, who
died during her second birth-giving. That fact renders the
genealogy tricky.

The Boyles grandfather taught me how to plow behind a
mule.

Grandfather later had a heart attack while we twins were
in college in Georgia. We took time off from school, came
home and nursed him through what would be his last illness.
The nursing included a much enjoyed daily barber-shop type
shave with straight razor by his cowhand grandson. His death
was followed by health deterioration for Grandmother. She
lived her last years being cared for by Mother in our home.

Back home at Island Grove it wasn't all work and no play.
There were frequent swimming trips to Simmons pond and
occasionally to Orange Springs. Orange Springs had cooler
water and more shade but was nearly 14 miles away. We made
the trips in the rumble seat of our Model A Ford. The newer
1937 two-door Chevrolet sedan was more reliable but a bit
stodgy for Nelline's and my taste. Besides, you could better
view the majesty of God's world from the rumble seat of a

Model A. Shopping trips to Ocala and Gainesville were made in the Chevrolet, as were an occasional trip to the circus in Jacksonville.

A visit to the circus had one small downside and that was having to wear a chunk of foul-smelling asafetida on a string around the neck to ward off any germs circulated by the city people. My mother never said it, but I surmise that she believed city people were more likely to contract disease from lack of fresh air, sunshine, fresh nutritional food and hard work. If that be true certainly they were more likely to transmit disease for the simple reason they lived so close to each other. During those trips I observed that the closeness of their neighbors surely deprived them of the rite of passage of the southern male to urinate in the backyard. I suspected that this rite was akin to the instinct of male dogs to urinate on a bush or automobile tire.

During the time Nelline and I were eight to ten years of age the Stallings family occasionally visited our family for what I remember to be long weekends, and of course they stayed in our house. Jimmy and Wallace Stallings were sons of Cleo and Council Stallings. Cleo was a daughter of Jeater and his first wife Lula, who was, as I indicated, a sister to Grandma Nellie.

Being raised in the country, I always carried a folding pocket knife as essential to many necessary tasks. A pocket knife was used to scale or skin fish, skin and butcher game, whittle, trim and clean finger nails and carve initials in trees. Over time one became adept in its use and this adeptness was the origin of the sport of mumbly peg.

Mumbly peg was apparently not known in north Georgia where the Stallings lived. Mumbly peg was played with two players. A flip of a coin determined who went first. The game was played with three turns at five progressively harder steps. In step one the knife was placed on the front of a closed fist and, with a curving motion, thrown to the ground. Landing upright with the blade in the ground permitted the player to take the knife by the blade and "hammer" the mumbly peg, a pre-selected straight limb about 3/8" in diameter and about five inches long which had been placed upright with about one inch in the ground. A successful strike drove the peg deeper in the ground. Failing to get the knife upright gave the opponent his turn.

Step two involved one knee on the ground with the other calf upright. The point of the knife was placed vertically on the upright knee and with the forefinger on top of the handle the knife was put in motion hopefully to land upright with the blade in the soil. The final step included holding the knife horizontal at eye level with the blade between the fore and middle fingers. Its descent to the ground took place when the fore and middle finger were simply separated. The winner was the first one to complete all three chances at the fifth step. A good player could at this point have the top of the peg at an inch or two below grade. The loser simply had to lie on his belly and use nothing but nose and mouth to unearth the peg.

The Georgia cousins never won but they tried, tried and tried. Mumbly peg was a spectator sport because few spectacles matched the groaning, spitting and nostril cleaning of the loser in retrieving the peg. Retrieval also revealed a sooty-like face clenching a 5-inch peg between its teeth.

Jimmy later obtained a PhD in theology and became a Baptist preacher. I would not have told the mumblypeg thing but I knew Jimmy had told it from the pulpit at least three times. He preached my mother's funeral in 1982 and told it there. He was at one time pastor of Nelline's church and told it there when we attended one Sunday. Finally Nelline told me that he told it in 1999 when some of her children were attending his current church. He apparently indicated that he was kin to these visitors and that they had an uncle who was a Circuit Judge in Florida. The uncle, he said, should be in jail for the abuse he had heaped on his Georgia cousins.

I must confess that hearing Jimmy preach from the pulpit was an humbling experience. I had to add a family member to the list of better speakers than I. Maybe the humbling experience of the mumbly peg games contributed to the sense of humor necessary to his oratory.

Two examples are evidence of my mother's uncommon goodness. Our neighbors included Chet and Helen Crosby, their son and twin girls. The girls contracted spinal meningitis. They needed help. Zelma Cason (later to sue Ms. Rawlings) and my mother entered the home and were quarantined. They were confined to the home until the illness had run its course or taken its toll. Daily, Mama tacked a list of things needed on the front gate. After a lapse in time, Ms. Rawlings retrieved the list and gathered the things needed. She then delivered the food and medicine to the front gate and after another lapse in time Mother would take the supplies into the house. They were there to comfort, succor and nurse. I think it lasted three to four weeks. One twin died and one survived.

The ordeal over, Mama walked home to avoid contaminating the car. Daddy met her in the back yard where she shed her clothes. Daddy then lifted the clothes with a stick and went to the woods where he burned them. Then Mother, in the yard, got the luxury of a hot water bath with a strong disinfectant. Doing unto others had been done.

The second example involved the operation of the store. About half the sales were on some kind of credit and it was not infrequent that a circumstance like a lost job or new child rendered a customer unable to pay some or all of the debt. They needed not fret as Miss Corinne would always forgive some or all of the debt. Those truly in need knew they would have food.

My sister and I accompanied Miss Corinne to the trial of Cason vs. Rawlings. Mama was friends with both. The trial was on the claim by Ms. Cason that Ms. Rawlings invaded her privacy when she essentially wrote in Cross Creek that Zelma Cason was her profane friend. It was my first entrance into a courtroom. Whether the trial was a motivator for my choice of career I do not know. Ms. Kate Walton, co-counsel and daughter to attorney J.V. Walton, represented Ms. Cason. The case created an enormous precedent in the law concerning privacy. I later came to know "Miss Kate" as an exceptionally intelligent and skilled attorney and a strong-willed, well-spoken, well-mannered, loving and friendly woman. She was a true lady and became a true friend. Fifteen years later my wife became the second of a trio of strong-willed women who prevented the blooming of my genetic instincts for chauvinism. Miss Kate would become the third. When we later became law partners she allowed that she had indeed noticed the nattily dressed twins at the Cason/Rawlings trial.

My schooling began in the two-room school house when I was five. The first day Mama drove us to school and as soon as her car left the parking lot Nelline and I, with me leading, followed her home on foot. We were spanked and carried back and that trauma was repeated five times. I was to learn later that I had a reputation for being stubborn and persistent.

Once I became resigned to attending I immediately liked

school and became an excellent student. Grades one through four were in one room and were taught by Ms. Inez P. Rainwater. I was entertained by wondering if she ever referred to her name using her surname preceded by the two initials. Grades five, six and seven were in the other room and were taught by Ms. Benson. I graduated valedictorian of the seventh grade out of a class of seven. The eighth and ninth grades included a bus ride to Hawthorne. I won the American Legion Award upon completion of the eighth grade and was a fervent member of Future Farmers of America (FFA). I grew some crops and raised livestock and my days of following my roots and becoming a rural farmer in this heavenly land did not seem far away.

This would not be. My father was over draft age but volunteered for the World War II Army when I was about nine years old. One year later he was killed in action shortly after having fought in the Battle of the Bulge. During the battle, his unit served under General Patton and fought in the breakout. The devastation to his surviving wife and children seemed to be total. Only time and faith would make our loss bearable.

The devastation was made worse because my father's body was not returned until sometime in late 1949. It was almost as if he had walked away and not returned. The interment was in a national cemetery, Fort Barranacas, located within the Pensacola Naval Air Station. The funeral was military with taps but for me there was not complete closure.

During the spring of 2000 my wife and I drove to New Orleans for a wedding and, en route, we visited his grave site. While we were there they had a military funeral with taps. I completely lost it but it felt good. After fifty years, closure had to be done. My lovely wife began to lead the way.

My father's death was also an economic loss that had to be addressed. We were left dependent on the family savings, the store income and a $39 per month death benefit. As administrator of my mother's estate I later learned that not a penny of the death benefit had ever been spent. It went to the bank for hard times that never came.

I started going directly to the store after school and did the lifting of anything over twenty-five pounds, which included 100-pound sacks of flour and livestock feed. I did the stocking and pumped the gas. Mrs. Rawlings always tipped me a dime for pumping her gas. Part-time employees were no longer needed. At home the ladies did the cooking, kept the house and washed the dishes. I mowed the yards and cut the firewood, and I suspected that I would soon be as deft with an axe as my grandfather instructor. We were prospering while coping with our great loss, but I was still a fatherless war orphan.

My mother remarried when Nelline and I were thirteen and our stepfather, Leslie Bennett Pigue, soon became Chief of Police of Crescent City, Florida. Shortly thereafter we twins, kicking and screaming, were moved to Crescent City. Our roots were painfully severed. Island Grove was history and the Rickenbaker grandparents were almost forty miles away. Woe were we.

2

High school - college - law school
and a mate

Crescent City was in the southern part of Putnam county and, while much larger than Island Grove, it was and is still a small town. It had amenities not found in Island Grove and they included a bank, hardware stores, a drug store with soda fountain and a restaurant among others. We had to learn how to pay for groceries and we learned to tolerate the inconvenience of having a separate feed store. The town even had a traffic light and it bordered on Lake Crescent, a magnificent body of water. Nelline and I had to admit that the town was probably more user-friendly for teenagers.

We rented a large house on the outskirts of town with a sufficiently large and secluded backyard to handle nature calls. I assumed the city dwellers were having to leave what they were doing, go to the back door, brush their feet, enter the house, go to the bathroom, and retrace their steps to where they had been. The house sat within a five-acre orange grove which assured fresh fruit in the fall and winter and the aroma of orange blossoms in March. The twins, Nelline and I, tabled for the moment our plot to run away and move back home with Grandma. We mounted my newly-purchased used Cushman motor scooter and checked out the ever-important surroundings.

We explored Satsuma, Welaka, Georgetown, Seville, Pierson and other near-by places. I could tell by the habitat that the area contained the same game found in *The Yearling* areas. I shortly discovered that the waters of Lake George, Lake Crescent and the St. Johns river contained species of fish not found in *The Yearling* lakes because they were brackish. The waters were less muddy than the landlocked lakes around Island Grove because they were ever moving. They had a tidal influence. There were woods of pine and hardwood and farms, ranches, pastures and livestock. Lake Stella, a clear water lake, bordered the town limits and provided excellent swimming from a public dock. I was baptized in its waters and became a Junior Deacon in the First Baptist Church of Crescent City. The surroundings were just too beautiful to justify a run-away. We aborted the plan and visited the grandparents often. Two to three weeks later we were both totally hooked on the town, its people and its surroundings and Island Grove became a sweet memory.

Crescent City and the new stepfather slowly returned happiness and normalcy to Miss Corinne and her twins. The death of my father and no remarriage would likely have changed boy to man before it was time. I grew very fond of "Pa" and I knew that the affection was mutual. He later became a doting grandfather to my children. Meanwhile he had a boat and motor and bird dogs and I quail hunted and fished with him and other friends. I roamed and camped in the woods, worked part-time and soon traded the scooter for a Model A Ford. My pocket money insured that the carefree days were back and even better. We twins blossomed at Crescent City High School and both made excellent grades. Nelline played basketball on the school team and I played basketball, football and baseball. I was captain of the baseball and basketball teams and co-captain of the football team. Pa would come to the games whenever and wherever we played. The guilt of "replacing" my blood father was sometimes more than I could handle. I wrongfully chose to deal with it at a later time. The later date only came during the penning of these memoirs!

I became interested in girls and my sister, a cheerleader, would tell me which, if any, of the cheerleaders were interested in me. It worked well having a twin sister on the inside as I knew the answer would be "yes" when I asked for a date.

There was a strange encounter at the city dock during the summer before my senior year. I was standing in the middle of several cheerleaders my age enjoying the view that cheerleaders' clothes do not permit when suddenly "Bones" Jackson, a skinny little redheaded girl of eleven, pierced the group, kicked me in the shin and simultaneously said, "You think you're hot s__t, don't you." My response was delayed because I was trying to determine how she read my mind. I was after all a team leader in high school sports, had my own car and pocket money and had been voted best looking of the senior class, as was my sister. During the delay one of the cheerleaders responded that she would call Bones' mother, and that likely would result in the interior of Bones' mouth being washed with soap. Bones then kicked the cheerleader and advised her that she should do it and then talk about it. Bones, without further comment, sped to the next shin victim. Bones was Sara Mero Jackson. We had no meaningful contact for seven years, but we were to be married in eight. We produced four perfect children who have produced nine perfect grandchildren.

Those heavenly days ended too soon. I graduated from high school in June of 1952 and entered the University of Florida in September. Nelline also entered but she was not sure about her educational goals. I was sure that I would obtain a forestry degree and return to Crescent City and be paid for roaming the woods.

The burden of my parents' legacies was mostly offset by the pride. The burden included marriage, children/grandchildren, hard work, honest behavior, a productive role in society and doing unto others together with like observance of the other ten commandments. It would permit no divorce or spoiled misbehaving children. The exact weight of the burden was a subject I was disinclined to assess. I was young, having good times and knew that the measure of the actual burden was my Maker's decision, not mine. My Maker gave me a furlough but I knew the time would come to assume the burden.

The furlough lasted seven good years but the forty years to follow allowed no drifts to the slow lane. The first year of college was about basics and improving study skills. We twins did well, and though in different housing, still had close contact. There were many weekends at home and weekends at home meant that I postponed learning how to do laundry. I now know why Mother had indulged in the luxury of hiring her laundry done.

The second year went poorly. Nelline had enrolled in the x-ray technician school at Emory University in Atlanta. For almost twenty years, we had been figuratively joined at the hip and just as she had followed me from school that first day in Island Grove I followed her to school in Atlanta. It was a mistake. Following people to the restroom after a barium enema simply did not work for me and I returned to the University of Florida. My studies went well, dating girls went well and draft beer was ten cents for a large glass. I was careful that none of my money coming from Mother was ever used to buy beer. Somehow she would have known and there would have been sanctions.

Nelline, at about the time she graduated from Emory, ruffled the family feathers. She wrote Mother that she would soon marry Joel Roy Landress. Joel Roy was a several-generations native of Gwinett County, Georgia, was in the Air Force, and was stationed at Eglin Air Force Base in the panhandle of Florida. This much we knew from the letter but we were unsure of why Nelline had not required that he follow the tradition of asking for her hand. I knew that Miss Corinne was upset and probably livid or at least as livid as her personality would permit. I assumed that she would call the wedding off or at least impose sanctions. She surprised me and announced that she, myself and the two aunts present at our birth would attend the wedding. We did and returned home. Roy and Nelline ultimately produced for her four beautiful and gifted grandchildren. Roy moved into the circle of my closest friends and I became Grandfather "Jeater" to my nephews and nieces. The entire extended family knew that if you had a real problem you carried it to "Jeater". I later wondered if the rightness of the marriage had been revealed to Mother during prayer.

I returned to Gainesville and entered the School of Forestry. My furlough was nearing the half-way point and within several weeks I knew that forestry would not be. During my first two years all my elective courses had been in Arts, not Sciences. They included word study, philosophy, comparative religions, English history and American history. They were fascinating and on course to an understanding that what I should be, depended on who I was, and that, in turn, greatly depended on where I came from environmentally and genetically.

I then knew that the courtroom scene of *Cason vs Rawlings* probably would not have occurred if King John had not been forced to sign the *Magna Carta* at Runnymede. I knew that my southeastern roots included substantial Irish roots. The Irish roots, in turn, included Celtic roots which had been fused with Danish, Anglo-Saxon and Norman blood. My ancestors were Catholic or Anglican or both. I knew that the English language changed as a result of the Norman invasion. I realized that the birth of the United States was an uncommon event in history and that it would not have happened without great sacrifices by great men. My father's enlistment was a colonist doing unto others (the Queen's people and others) so that they could be free. I knew that he was a hero and a great man. I realized that the Constitution guarantees life, liberty, property and the pursuit of happiness absent misbehavior and that courts and juries enforce those rights and determine misbehavior. I needed to know more of those things and they were not included in the curriculum of Forestry. The semester was over and I switched to Political Science as a better background for law school.

My Bachelor of Arts degree came at the end of the summer session of 1957 and summer session in law school was now necessary if I was to complete law school before my furlough ended. My hedonistic days were rapidly fading and this twin had become a man. The man needed a mate and a decision on what to do with a law degree.

I entered law school in September, 1957 with one hundred-twenty-four other white males of whom only thirty-two would graduate. Florida Law School in those days was almost totally conceptual, mainly dealt with Common Law and there was little effort at teaching how to get disputes to the courtroom. There was no moot court then. There was a saying that 'A' students became law professors, 'B' students became judges and 'C' students made money. I now suspect that is partly true and it probably explained the lack of effort in training for practice. A great many of the professors had never practiced. They were academics. Not to worry, Miss Kate Walton Engelken, a country lawyer, would later show me the way. Practice under the Uniform Code of Military Justice I would have to learn on my own.

Law School required more study which resulted in less time for beer and ladies. I attended two summer schools and graduated in January instead of June of 1960. Miss Corinne and Pa were proud and pleased.

During early law school I was concerned about making no headway in finding a mate. Miss Corinne wanted grandchildren and I concurred that they were desirable and necessary. During my junior year my room-mate, William Wallace Smith, Jr, asked that I be in his wedding which would be at a Catholic church in Fort Lauderdale. During the pre-wedding festivities I was paired with a nineteen-year-old Irish lassie generically referred to as "Colleen" in these memoirs. She was about five feet five inches tall and had robin's-egg blue eyes framed in a Mediterranean complexion. The combination was striking when coupled with a perfect body and the whole package a sure head turner. It turned mine and I was instantly and strongly interested. Maybe the mate search was over. I pondered on whether Miss Corinne would permit a Catholic grandson. I had learned from Nelline's mistake. I knew within thirty minutes that the attraction was mutual and we were side by side all evening. Blue eyes gazed into blue eyes, both sets being mounted in Mediterranean complexions.

Following the wedding reception we donned bathing suits and swam in the ocean. Her body was more perfect than a dress could ever reveal and I wondered if I could be in love this quickly.

Serious courtship followed and that included several months of weekends in Lauderdale and Colleen spending some weekends in Gainesville. Whether we were seeing anyone else or "going steady" was never mentioned. I was not and couldn't imagine she was. We were not engaged and marriage had not been mentioned. We did, however, discuss the direction of my career. I was about ready to ask her father for her hand.

The courtship strained my time and money resources and I needed to do more studying and earn more money. Mother and Pa had purchased thirty-three acres on Lake Crescent and the acreage included a citrus grove and fishing resort where help was always needed. I had a standing invitation to be employed and earn extra money. I went home for the two-week Christmas holidays, worked during the day, and studied at night. That was December, 1958.

On my first day home I took the night off to go to Cooks restaurant to eat a hamburger, see old friends and go to a high school basketball game. Both places allowed old friends to see how scholarly, suave and debonnaire SLB had become. I was in Cooks eating and chatting with an old family friend when in walked Bones Jackson. Bones was now eighteen, had added flesh in exactly the right amounts and places and was as beautiful as Colleen but in a different way. Her sparkly blue eyes were set among some muted freckles and her red hair was a heavenly shade of auburn. Her features were near perfect in form and color and she was animated, spirited and bubbly while at the same time very poised. Brenau Academy, a finishing school for girls in Gainesville, Georgia and nature had made the shin-kicker into a very, very lovely young lady.

My head had been turned twice in less than a year and it was causing me extreme discomfort. Fate was out of my hands when my friend suggested that the lady deserved an escort to the game. It would be ungentlemanly to refuse since we were both headed to the same place. My discomfort came from the sure knowledge that attending the game with this instant attraction could endanger my very special relationship with my very special Colleen. It did. I returned to law school knowing that this would be the one. The second most painful moment of my life would be telling Colleen. It had to be done and it was painful.

The next summer I asked James Mann Jackson for his daughter's hand and he agreed. In a separate traditional ritual (on my knees at her knee) she agreed. The other twin had a mate and my furlough was nearly over. James Mann Jackson died that August at the age of 54. We were married at Holy Comforter Episcopal Church (in Crescent City) exactly one year from our "chance" encounter and toured Florida for the honeymoon. I had on hand less than two hundred dollars. I later learned that as she passed Cooks restaurant she recognized my car, did a U-turn under the traffic light and entered the restaurant. She did not tell me how she knew it was my car and I equate that to a confession that I had been stalked.

We returned to Gainesville, rented an apartment for one month and I graduated on January 30, 1960, still absent an ultimate goal. I had applied for a position as Special Agent with the FBI as I had developed a real interest in criminal law and believed that street-level enforcement experience would be valuable. Pa, upon purchasing the fishing resort, had become a part-time constable and I often rode with him searching for fugitives. I remember one occasion we arrived at a house believed to contain a fugitive. Pa posted me at the back door and he took position at the front door. I had no weapon so I shouted around the house, "Pa, what do I do if he comes out the back door?" Pa's reply was two words: "Stop him!"

Miss Sara's father was the part-time Justice of the Peace and I noted that he and Pa would occasionally exceed their jurisdiction to achieve justice. Their only jurisdiction in felony crimes was to effect an arrest and hold a preliminary hearing to determine if there was probable cause to bind the matter over to Circuit Court. It was more often the case that a first offense felony involving no victim injury would be disposed of by a report to the parents coupled with a period of "proba- tion" under the supervision of the Constable. These were two good, honest and well-intended men and they achieved good results. They were the law south of Dunns Creek. This was my first experience in the criminal justice system. I wondered why I was uneasy with the concept.

I surmised that working for the FBI would allow us to see another part of the country since new agents were not then stationed in the region of their origin. I knew we would re- turn to Florida when grandchildren time came. I add that "The Untouchables," featuring Elliott Ness, was at that time my favorite TV show.

3

Lawyer enters USAF and becomes
First Lieutenant in JAG

We returned to Crescent City to await the results of the FBI application and moved in with Miss Sara's mother, Florence, and her mother's sister, Mayme. They hired me to paint the house and in late March or early April the background investigator arrived and explained that I was accepted subject to draft status. We drove to Palatka to check the status and discovered that my 2-S school deferment had been changed to 1-A on the day I graduated from law school. My draft papers were already in the Palatka office.

The investigating agent thanked me for the application and left. There would be no FBI. The Palatka draft office graciously offered to hold the papers for one week so that I might decide between the Army and other armed services. The Army would be two years but the others (enlistments) were four. They updated my status to include the marriage and explained that a pregnancy would exempt me from service. They also said that the sole surviving son of a father killed during wartime could claim non-combatant service.

Miss Sara was, in fact, pregnant but her condition had not been medically confirmed. I returned home a troubled man knowing that the son of Lloyd and Corinne could not claim either exemption and tarnish his father's legacy. My only option was to serve four years in another branch hopefully in positions that would be career-enhancing. I suspected that this news might not be well-received by my new bride and I then already knew she would not tolerate arbitrariness. This had the potential for a marital dispute and I had no experience in such matters. The kinder and gentler days were over. Maybe there would be more later but for now the furlough had ended.

The news was not received joyously. The only approach I was able to develop carried substantial risk and our discussions centered only on the pain and unhappiness it would cause me to dishonor my father's legacy (I confirm later that my self-esteem would not have survived intact if I had opted for either exemption). I did not say that for me there was only one option. Her concurrence, or at least acquiescence, would be necessary to avoid a serious impasse. This was a strong-willed woman and we were already doing most things her way. She acquiesced and I was greatly relieved. The decision resulted in solid bedrock for career enhancement.

The United States Air Force (USAF) was then giving direct First Lieutenant commissions to graduates of accredited law schools who had been admitted to the Bar. I had taken the Bar exam but would not receive the results until late May. I had learned from a mandatory 2-year ROTC stint that dress wear for Air Force officers included blue oxford cloth shirts which could be worn with little or no starch. My decision was made. I would enlist in the Air Force and if I passed the Bar would apply for the commission. Passing the Bar was not a given. Graduates of Stetson and The University of Miami averaged about a 70 per cent rate for first time takers and Florida graduates had about an 85 percent pass rate. Failing the Bar would leave only one option and that would be Officer Training School which could result in a Second

Lieutenant's commission. Options would then include pilot training or training in other fields such as the Air Police.

On April 26, 1960 my bride drove me to Jacksonville where I had a physical and took the oath. I was an Airman Basic in the Air Force. The separation from Miss Sara being imminent, I wondered if I had done the right thing. My bride was in pain and I was in pain as I boarded the bus and we were driven to the airport for a flight to Lackland Air Force Base near San Antonio, Texas. Our group arrived at our assigned barracks and at about 4 a.m. we wearily went to bed. At 5 a.m. we were roused out of bed, cursed, and belittled. Showing a slight semblance of a formation, we marched to the chow hall. The food was good. The darkest day was over. I was selected Barracks Chief and with that came a private room and no latrine duties. Basic training went well. I was strong, athletic, and as the son of Corinne already knew discipline. I was already familiar with firearms and had no problem adapting to Air Force weapons. I was amused at the difficulties encountered by the city boys in learning to shoot.

Late in May my Technical Instructor (TI) said that I should call home. The telegram had arrived. I had passed the Bar exam and needed only to be sworn in. I went to the orderly room and applied for emergency leave to return home. The Squadron Commander, doubtless never having seen a similar request, declined the leave. I then went to the Staff Judge Advocate office and requested permission to see an Assistant Staff Judge Advocate. I was permitted to see Lt. Col. "Robbie" Robertson. I explained my plight and found that he too was a Florida lawyer from Deland, Florida only thirty miles from Crescent City. He opined that being sworn in at the Supreme Court of Florida was the only real way to go. He said he would discuss the leave with my commander. The next morning I received his message that the leave had been approved and that the new Commander of McCoy Air Force Base would be leaving that afternoon for Orlando. "Did I want a ride" and please come see him when I returned and he would help with the direct commission application. That afternoon I went to the flight line and climbed on board the general's aircraft. I was the only other passenger and I chatted with the general and wondered if the military might be my career choice.

Miss Sara picked me up at McCoy. I had learned several weeks before that the pregnancy was confirmed and Leslie Lynn Boyles would be born on January 5, 1961. It was a happy reunion with the wife and my parents and on June 6, 1960 I was sworn in at the Supreme Court of Florida. I had never ridden on a train so I selected that as the mode of transportation to return to Texas. Because of the connections I had about two hours to tour Bourbon Street in New Orleans. Bourbon Street appeared to be populated solely by people two and three times my age but none appeared to have been emancipated from hedonism.

Lt. Col. Robertson got the application moving. The process took some time because the personnel people involved were unsure that you could go from slick-sleeve to silver in one step. Meantime I completed basic training and Col. Robertson arranged that I temporarily become a medical/dental records clerk at squadron level. I was housed in a nearby barracks and, at work, was under the supervision of First Sergeant Jesse Dinkins. He and I became friends. He graciously enhanced my education on what the military was all about and carefully explained a major list of things to avoid. I suspected from my observations in the orderly room that the Air Force could not operate without First Sergeants. I became convinced that the Squadron Commander who denied my leave would think I had jumped rank. I stayed clear of his squadron. I seldom saw the Squadron Commander Sgt. Dinkens served.

On August 8 I was Honorably Discharged from non-commissioned service. On August 9, I was commissioned as a First Lieutenant and became an officer and a gentleman by Direction of the President. Col. Robertson suggested that uniform-wise I could get by with severing the new stripe from the sleeve and simply acquiring an officer's overseas cap and sufficient insignia of rank for the cap and collars. These were khaki known as "505s" and they had to be starched. Dress blues with the soft cotton blue shirts were my first priority. He told me that purchasing uniforms was done at the beginning of the Legal/Chaplin School to which I would be assigned. That school was located across the base and its purpose was to acquaint directly-commissioned officers in the ways of the military. The course was mostly about military history, military protocol and wearing of the uniform which was somewhat repetitious for me. During the day of uniform buying I had to explain to several that you couldn't buy the service hat with the scrambled eggs (bright yellow embroidery)until you became a field grade officer. I then had to explain that a field grade officer in the Air Force was Lt. Colonel or higher.

Col. Robertson finally called and said that my first duty assignment had been made. I was only mildly curious because Miss Sara and I had agreed on requesting an assignment at McCoy in Orlando, Tyndall in Panama City or Patrick in Cocoa. Any one of these would provide frequent home visits and grandparent access. The Colonel stated that it was with the 4081st Combat Support Group located at Ernest Harmon AFB in Stephenville, Newfoundland, Canada. I responded with an appreciative laugh because we were now friends enough to joke around. I was promptly told that he was dead serious and that no dependency travel could be authorized until we had been approved for off-base housing. I still remember Miss Sara's laugh when I called her with the news. Her reaction was identical to the "joke" foisted on me by Col. Robbie. We separately found global maps as we did not know where Newfoundland was. It would, career-wise, develop as the assignment of choice. Personally it would be a life experience worth handing down and provide a close-up look at what Anglo-Saxons were doing in the western North Atlantic. Oh we of little faith! Strategic Air Command was where the action was and that was especially true for overseas installations.

On August 9 I performed an amazing feat for the barracks guard. He knew I had gone to bed the night before as an Airman Third Class. The next morning as I approached the door in my First Lieutenant uniform he responded with a startled "Tennn-hut!" and saluted. I handed him the traditional dollar bill and was amused by the thought that had Bones observed the scene it would have been, "You think you're hot s__t, don't you!" Right again. The Citra-born Airman Basic had risen to Officer/Gentleman status in only 104 days. I completed the curriculum at the Legal/ Chaplin School and took a delay en route leave to fly home.

The bad day at the bus station had not been forgotten. The "no dependency travel authorized" clause in my assignment order was not a bar to dependent accompaniment. It was frowned upon but legally it meant there would be no pay for the travel of the dependent and household goods could not be moved at government expense. I knew that the tour with dependents would be thirty-six months and the tour without dependents would be eighteen. We both agreed, without discussion, that a tour "without" was not an option. My upbringing included the tradition that the maternal grandmother should be present for the birth of grandchildren. The decision came easily. We would drive to Newfoundland and Miss Florence would be our companion. She was, after all, an avid traveler. She and her sister Mayme had traveled to Europe many times. She had never traveled to Newfoundland.

4

Lieutenant, wife and her mother travel to Newfoundland

We left Crescent City on October 1, 1960. I did not then know Miss Florence that well. That would change. Mayme died in the early eighties and we later enclosed our carport to provide Miss Florence with living quarters and an antique shop. Her final days were spent in the main part of the house as the "Queen Mother." She was a welcome addition to the trip as Miss Sara was very pregnant and tended to be car-sick. Ninety percent of the time she was asleep on the back seat and the left-over ten percent was reserved primarily for frequent pit stops. Florence developed a basket which contained a canteen of coffee, sandwiches and assorted other goodies. We early on learned that eating in a restaurant would only occur when it coincided with a pit stop. Things went more smoothly when Miss Sara was not awakened.

Our route included some time on the Blue Ridge Parkway as I had never spent any real time in the mountains and I was in awe of this version of God's nature. We chatted (mostly Miss Florence), nibbled food and drove on. We spent the third night at the Mero sisters' summer cottage in West Buxton, Maine, where they spent most summers buying antiques which they shipped or carried to their "Three Sisters Antique Shop" in Crescent City. The next day was the peak of the fall colors and it was beautiful beyond description and together with the cool dry weather, exhilarating. We continued on through Bar Harbor, Maine, and I noted that this must be the highest rent district in the country and that it probably was only inhabited by bluebloods. I would shortly meet one of them. We traveled through New Brunswick into Nova Scotia and arrived at North Sydney, Nova Scotia. We boarded the ferry "William Carson" and ninety or so miles later we docked at Port au Basque and, through the port-hole, I saw shards and shivers of ice hitting the deck. I assumed they were icing fish for the trip back to Sydney. On deck we observed that we were in a sleet storm and there were no fish. Miss Sara was not happy.

We drove on to Stephenville and a caution sign at one point indicated that winds frequently gusted to 160 miles an hour. The sleet storm had not subsided as we entered Ernest Harmon AFB. The village of Stephenville did not impress Miss Sara and her look indicated that she had been unwillingly thrust to the end of the earth. At the Visiting Officers' Quarters (VOQ) we took two rooms which only accommodated sleeping and sitting. It was to be home for sixty days. A recent web site possibly and belatedly lends some support to Miss Sara's version of the "Rock". The island was commonly referred to as the "Rock" and I knew that Miss Sara considered it to have many Alcatraz-like characteristics. Portions of the website **www.excite.com/travel/countries/newfoundland/** are as follows:

> "Newfoundland may not be the edge of the world, but it sure seems like it; wind-whipped grass, murky fog, rocky cliffs plunging into the wild sea. It's a place where, we walk slower than usual, making sure there's solid ground under each footstep. . . Geographically the province often confuses visitors, as it is made up of both an island (Newfoundland proper)and a portion of mainland Canada (La-

brador). The island is often referred to as "the Rock" and Labrador either as"the Mainland" or "the Labrador."

5

Lieutenant reports for duty

The next morning I went to Base Headquarters for the 4081st Combat Support Group and learned that we supported the 4081st Strategic Wing, a part of the Eighth Air Force which was a part of the Strategic Air Command. Down a hallway I walked into the office of the Staff Judge Advocate. The Non-Commissioned Officer In Charge, usually referred to as NCOIC, escorted me to the office of Major Oscar H. Emery, Jr. The NCOIC said that the Major was from Bar Harbor, Maine, had WWII service as a navigator on a B-17 bomber, had been recalled for the Korean conflict and decided to stay. I suspected that I was about to meet a true silk stocking lawyer warrior of the blueblood variety. I did. The NCOIC had also gratuitously noted that the Major had a pretty strong bark but did little biting. The NCOIC and I had bonded. That was good. Somehow I knew that he knew that I was not a typical graduate of the Legal/Chaplain school.

I knocked twice on the door and announced that Boyles, Lieutenant, requested permission to enter. Permission was granted. I walked briskly to the front of his desk, came to rigid attention, saluted and held the salute until it was returned. There was some hesitation in the return and I instantly knew why. He had supervised other Lieutenant graduates of the Legal/Chaplain School whose first encounter with the boss included a casual stroll into his office without knocking and the offer of a handshake. Their uniforms and the wearing were deficient in many respects. They had little military bearing and were only there because they had to put in their time. I knew that during the hesitation he was scrutinizing for a flaw. There were none. The insignia was properly located, the gig line was perfectly aligned, the pants length permitted the proper slight break in the seam atop the shoe, the metal at the end of the belt allowed no blue between it and the belt buckle and the shoes were spit shined. He sharply returned the salute and gestured that I sit.

His first impression created the right moment to confess that my wife and mother-in-law had made the trip with me and were now in the Visiting Officers Quarters (VOQ). I perceived correctly. His only response was that adequate off-base housing was hard to come by. The transgression was forgiven.

The similarities between this man and myself were striking considering our disparate backgrounds. Probably Anglo-Saxon roots were the only thing we shared. The similarities included the tieknot—a four-in-hand as opposed to the symmetrical Windsor—and the point of the overlap properly touching, but not overlapping, the belt buckle. The four-in-hand included a small dimple centered on the overlay at the bottom of the horizontal portion of the knot. It was usually referred to as a DA (duck's ass). The knot offsets a touch of boredom caused by total symmetry created by the Windsor. I would shortly help elect, by absentee ballot, a new Commander-in-Chief of lace curtain Irish descent, a WWII Navy hero and a Catholic who preferred the four-in-hand. I later read an article suggesting that women are much impressed by a neat collar with a four-in-hand. The days following revealed that the Major's and my views and values were akin. I had found another father.

The accumulation of about twelve years' worth of life and professional experiences were about to begin and would be completed in about thirty-two months. The Major explained that I would be the Claims Officer and in that capacity would adjudicate the value of loss and damage to personnel household shipments. As Claims Officer I would also investigate and recommend settlements for any damages deemed caused by the Air Force to Newfoundlanders and their property. I learned that Newfoundland was properly pronounced New-fun-land. The NCOIC and I would inspect off-base housing and approve or disapprove according to Air Force guidelines. The other Lieutenants in the office and I would be assigned by order of the Base Commander as either Trial Counsel (Prosecutor) or Defense Counsel in Special Courts Martial. The orders would also appoint members of the Court and set its convening date. The Base Commander was the convening authority but his orders convening Courts Martial were actually the work of the Staff Judge Advocate. My duties would also include reviewing for legal sufficiency the transcripts of other proceedings. An example was a Flying Evaluation Board (FEB) which had heard evidence and concluded that a pilot had fear of flying and should be taken off flying status.

The Major told me that the Manual for Courts Martial included the Uniform Code of Military Justice (UCMJ) and that both should be read word-by-word. The implication was that it would eliminate my asking him questions the answers to which could be found in the book. Finally, he said I would have other duties not related to legal affairs which would include Protocol Officer for one week of every six. The Protocol Officer was on call 24 hours a day during that week and his primary duty was to see to the needs of any full Colonel

or above who landed on the base. My Extended War Operation (EWO) duty would be Ramp Replenishment Monitor.
Our mission at the base was in-air refueling of B-52 bombers
by KC-97 tankers. The tanker was propeller-driven and ran
on gasoline. The bomber was a jet and ran on JP-4, a fuel
similar to kerosene. Refueling the tanker meant getting the
right fuel in the right amount in the right tank. This was overseen by the Monitor.

I was shown my desk and my in-basket indicated I would
prosecute my first case on Monday morning. The file revealed
that an Air Policeman had gotten drunk, broke open the barracks drink machine and stole the money. He was later appre-
hended in nearby Stephenville Crossing for another reason.
He was in a Newfoundlander's yard trying to steal his goose.
The amounts and kinds of change in his pockets made him a
suspect to the drink machine theft. He was interviewed by an
Air Police investigator and confessed. The problem was that
the investigator had signed in the space provided for the defendant and the defendant had signed in the space provided
for the investigator. I had no clue on the procedures involved
in a Court Martial but remembered the Major's direction. I
took the manual with me in order to have time for its complete reading before Monday morning and went to the VOQ
to comfort and succor Miss Sara's distress. Bringing Miss
Florence with us had been a wise decision. That weekend we
explored the contents of what Miss Sara believed to be the
end of the earth.

We got a map and drove to the nearby Port au Port Peninsula which lay north of St. George's Bay. That Bay became
the Gulf of St. Lawrence as you moved westerly. During the
coming February we could, if so inclined, walk across the
Gulf of St. Lawrence to Labrador which was part of New-

foundland. The bay froze solid to a depth of about six feet. The perimeter of Newfoundland was mostly jagged with steep cliffs and fiords which fell sharply to the sea. Moving slightly inland it was undulating and contained the Long Range Mountains which were an extension of the Appalachian Range but occasionally a single mountain rose sharply from its relatively flat surroundings. The island was heavily forested and included conifers and hardwoods. The conifers were mostly fir and spruce and the hardwoods were the same as found in the Appalachians of Maine. There were large and deep lakes with clear water. The center of the island was lower and flatter and contained substantial bogs. The bogs were probably created because the basin-like configuration of the island caused much of the surface water run-off to flow inland. It was rugged and remote but it was absolutely beautiful or said another way it was beautiful because it was rugged and remote. Miss Sara did not share my view.

An area named Lewis Hills included Cabox Mountain which rose to 2672 feet above sea level. It was the highest elevation in Newfoundland and lay about 10 miles north of Stephenville. Lt. Stephen Lewis Boyles was a far piece from home but surely he was living among blood kin. The Lieutenant's bride expressed the notion that this possibility was unlikely to increase her current comfort level. The mother-in-law uncharacteristically said nothing but her querulous expression indicated some concern that she had not yet observed the newlyweds share any view.

We limited the exploration that day to the Port au Port Peninsula. Miss Sara would not be riding that much until her pregnancy was over. I suspected that it mattered little to her because the places she wanted to visit were very few and she had some fear that if she went very far she would fall off the end of the earth. The peninsula was home mostly to lobster and cod fishermen. Drying cod were seen hanging on many clotheslines and there was an occasional small sheep ranch. The houses were mostly frame/clapboard and brightly colored in varied colors. These Anglo-Saxon kin were pursuing life more similar than dissimilar to those in Citra and Island Grove. They were farmers and fishermen but because of the climate they produced different table products.

The 1901 census revealed that Stephenville had 643 residents, only nine of whom were Protestant. During 1940 Newfoundland was a part of the British Commonwealth and in that year the Unites States leased 1859 acres adjacent to Stephenville. This acreage became Ernest Harmon AFB. Almost overnight the Stephenville population rose to about 7000. During 1949 Newfoundland became a province of Canada and Canada and the United States were both members of NATO. Differences in the lease provisions and the NATO provisions would later cause me great heartburn in matters of "jurisdiction."

We were en route home when we stopped at a country store to buy Miss Sara a cola which was retrieved from a shelf and sold. We noticed wooden barrels that contained both whole rabbits, with entrails still in, and seal flippers. Manufactured ice was not a necessity in this land. On July 2, 1962 at 1 p.m. the temperature would rise to 71 degrees and stay there for about twenty minutes. A record was set and the Newfoundlanders were sorely uncomfortable with the heat. I began to notice that I was more comfortable with real cold than with real heat but that it was not a condition shared by my bride. She decided to pass on the seal flippers since we did not have a kitchen (perhaps there was another reason?).

Returning home, we entered a banked curve to the left on

a falling grade. Ice on the road caused the vehicle to abruptly change lane and direction. On Miss Florence's animated exclamation concerning whether I intended to do that, I calmly replied that it might be shorter this way. So far as I knew it might have been and there was therefore no sinful lie to my mother-in-law. Her daughter was almost asleep on the back seat and we returned without further incident. I completed reading the Manual for Courts Martial which would not be far from my elbow for the next four years. I would have one at the office and one at quarters and the Monday coming I would not have procedural questions for the Major.

6

JAG Begins Duties and Finds Quarters — and a New Baby Girl

I arrived at my duty station about fifteen minutes before the prescribed hour of 7 a.m. Procedure for a Special Court was explicitly set out in the Manual and included a prescribed dialogue. Trial counsel, defense counsel and the President of the Court each performed their procedural role from the Manual. I had paid special attention to the uniform. The trial was to begin at 8 a.m. and my opponent arrived at 7:10 a.m. He was from Brooklyn, New York and had paid no attention to his uniform. He was putting in his time. The NCOIC, because of our bond, let me know that my adversary had read my personnel file. Teaching a "Bubba" a lesson would be fun and relieve his boredom. Yankees were much smarter than "Crackers."

I knew when we entered the courtroom that basic training had provided me with an advantage over these thinly disguised civilians. The members of the Court were for the most part career officers and many had served in WWII. Their uniforms and bearing were correct for true warriors. During my trial of this case I found that such proceedings were very formal. The evidence was presented and the arguments made. The Lieutenant with the poorly shined shoes and sloppy uniform was not able to sell the defense of signatures being in the wrong place. The Lieutenant with spit-shined shoes stood erect at the podium and appeared to be uncommonly conversant with the elements of larceny. He traced its roots to the Common Law of England and was either well-prepared or had had some life experience with the subject matter. Justice was almost as swift as the justice of Miss Corinne. The "verdict" took about ten minutes and sentence was imposed by 3:30 p.m. The Citra version of Clarence Darrow had won his first case. The theories were now rubber meeting road. The "smarter" Lieutenant should have urged the "drunk" defense on the element of intent. He did not. It might have worked because most WWII soldiers had been there.

During that same week I returned home and the ladies were having high tea with a lady guest. I was introduced and sat down. Miss Florence had met the lady at church and invited her over and I noticed that my bride was, indeed, a poised and well-mannered lady involving herself in the conversation only at appropriate times. I wondered if she would be so poised if she knew she was in the presence of the wife of the Vice Wing Commander. I was uncomfortable thinking that such an invitation might be a breach of protocol. I later disclosed the visit to Major Emery in terms that assured him that I had not been consulted on the invite. I also shortly would have to disclose to Miss Sara that an officer in uniform, walking with his lady, is not permitted to carry children or groceries. The reason is that he must walk erect with the left hand at the seam of the pants and the thumb covering the crease of the forefinger. The right hand must be free to salute or return salutes. The news was not well received. The response was a pre-Brenau shin-kicking assertion that cannot be printed.

During early December we moved into quarters. Quarters was an 8' x 32' trailer with a frame attachment and the attachment consisted of an 8'x8' rear "Master" bedroom and a small foyer which served double purposes; it allowed storage of the snow shovel and a place to park snow-laden shoes and top coats. Miss Florence was relegated to box springs and mattress at the rear of the trailer house. There was a small bath and kitchen but no laundry appliances. About a month later the bath tub primarily became a place to soak and wash diapers. There was no television so we could not watch hockey night in Canada and the Massey-Furguson Hour. On the upcoming January 5, 1961 Leslie Lynn was born and driven home in the Cadillac of the Vice Wing Commander. I was in trial. The delivery and hospital stay cost seven dollars. The government was not allowed to pay for the mother's hospital food. There had been no charge for the pre-natal care.

7

JAG ponders destiny and hunts ptarmigan

Six weeks after Leslie was born, Miss Florence flew home. She would return four times. Miss Sara and I made some friends who included Joseph J. Buser, Jr., his wife Jurdis, Patrick J. O'Toole and his wife Barbara. The Busers were from Texas and the O'Tooles from Massachusetts. Pat was in the Comptroller's Office and Joe was a Deputy Information Officer. He later sent an article to the weekly newspaper in Crescent City chronicling the military life and achievements of the former frog hunter. It made front page with a photo of the Lieutenant in uniform and SLB became something akin to a favorite son. Other friends included Roger Hagel, a helicopter pilot from Illinois and Chuck Cook, a doctor from Texas. Miss Sara now had a personal pediatrician and Roger became my hunting and handball partner.

During the early months of 1961 I suspected that Miss Sara and Miss Florence were conspiring for Miss Sara to hop a plane, carry the first-born home, annul the marriage and marry a sane lawyer. The lawyer she was married to was either a nutcake or retarded. He loved his job, loved the military, loved Newfoundland and had no inkling of how silly and foolish these protocol things were. I was often seen at the close of many busy duty days of prosecuting and defending in Courts Martial, voluntarily standing in front of base headquarters, at attention, saluting the lowering of the flag and listening to the wail of the bugle. Perhaps the wailing of the bugle was my siren and I knew not that it was shipwrecking my mind. I found quirks akin to those of General Patton and was beginning to feel a destiny of being in uniform. I thrived on wind, snow and cold; I trampled in hip-deep fresh snow to pursue caribou and ptarmigan. I believed that this forsaken and remote land was another fine example of God's Architecture.

I should have told Miss Sara that I had never heard a live bugle before my father's military funeral. Taps tore into my soul but it was the most beautiful thing I had heard or would ever hear. Hearing a bugle always reminded me of the pride in being the son of Lloyd. Exploring woods was genetic and a soothing furlough from responsibility. We did not really understand each other but we had been married only about a year.

On a weekend caribou hunt I was paired with a Mounty (Royal Canadian Mounted Policeman) who had a lame leg and because of the lameness did not stray far from the Jeep. On the return to Camp 33, an Air Force Recreation Camp located on the edge of Grand Lake, the Mounty pointed out Hare Hill and allowed that on the previous weekend he had climbed the mountain, bagged fourteen ptarmigan and returned to his Jeep in less than ninety minutes. I relayed the good news to my friend Roger and the next Saturday we exited my Jeep to climb Hare Hill. Hare Hill rose abruptly and steeply from its surroundings to an elevation of about eight hundred feet. It was shaped much like an inverted doodle bug home. It took us about four hours to ascend its summit and we were well-conditioned, young and not lame. Mounties may always get their man but at least one had lied. The summit was granite with only sparse vegetation and berry bushes in its crevices. There was not a feather to be found. We kicked at the vegetation and berry bushes but there was no flutter. It was fall and we were soon battered by a sudden sleet storm and the ice hitting our bare necks was too much to endure. There was then a saying among newfoundlanders, "If you don't like the weather wait five minutes and it will change". We tumbled down the steep slopes in slightly less than one hour. The planned ptarmigan feast would include only commissary chicken.

A recent Internet web site www.nf.sympatico.ca'cpelley/ harehill/ aptly describes the place:

> "Hare Hill is a prominent elevation in the Long Range Mountains of western Newfoundland. At 1957 feet above sea level, it commands an inspiring view of the surrounding wooded countryside. Wildlife sightings are common. Caribou graze on and around the summit, rock ptarmigan nest among the tuckamore and arctic hare have been known to live here.
>
> It is a wilderness area in every respect. There are no developed trails. The hillsides are crisscrossed by caribou trails and have been used for centuries, deeply etched into the landscape.
>
> This route is a one-day hike, covering 4 kilometers of wilderness, 800 feet elevation gain, 1957 above sea level. Seven kilometers over forest access road, no marked trails, moderate to difficult terrain, for expert map and compass navigators, experienced hikers."

Roger did some research. Ptarmigan in fact inhabited Newfoundland and were usually found at higher elevations like Lewis Hills. He scouted Lewis Hills with his helicopter and, from the experience with Hare Hill, estimated the climb would take eight to ten hours. There was not that much daylight in the fall and the climb would have to start before daylight and end after dark.

Another site *(www.stemnet.nf.ca/~cpelley/lewis01.htm)* aptly demonstrates that we had grossly underestimated the time to access Lewis Hills by foot:

> "At 815 meters above sea level the Lewis Hills are the highest on the island of Newfoundland. Sparkling streams, flowing from snow fields that persist throughout the summer, tumble and fall into 800 meter canyons! Arctic hare can be seen grazing the sparse vegetation among the boulders. Caribou seek relief from the summer heat on the snow fields. Moose raise their young in the secluded valleys of the lowlands. Ptarmigan, perfectly camouflaged, will scarcely move as you pass.
>
> "The Lewis Hills are accessible only on foot. Trails are nonexistent. The terrain is rugged and sturdy footwear is recommended. Since the altitude varies from sea level to over eight hundred meters, night temperatures dip low. A warm sleeping bag and extra layers of warm clothes are necessary to ensure comfort. The weather is unpredictable and can change very quickly. Waterproof and wind proof outer layers are essential. River crossings may be necessary and since there are no bridges, wading is the only alternative. Water levels may be high or low, depending on the time of year and local rainfall amounts. Water temperature may also vary from pleasantly cool to bone chilling cold."

Roger opined that he was sure he could be authorized a training mission which would allow hovering the copter over Lewis Hills while I descended the ladder and shot the ptarmigan. Miss Sara without hesitation declined Roger's offer. Having it her way was a windfall; I did not have to disclose or search for a reason other than cowardice to support my own disinclination. (During June, 2000 we located Roger on the Internet and called. He answered the phone and I inquired,

"Would the 'bye' [Newfoundlanders pronunciation for boy] be ready to go ptarmigan hunting?" He knew who it was and the conversation lasted well over an hour. He reckoned that the tour, on reflection and with the passage of time, was a real-life "MASH."

8

Life in the military on the "rock"

Back at the base I was prosecuting and defending many cases. One case included the defense of the NCOIC of base salvage. The NCOIC was a surviving member of the infamous Bataan death march of WWII and had chosen the eighteen-month tour without family. According to the file he became involved with a native woman and the involvement resulted in a shortage of cash. He sold surplus property to Newfoundlanders and pocketed the proceeds. He was caught and I was his assigned defense lawyer. I knew from experience that the defense would really focus on the avoidance of an almost-sure Bad Conduct Discharge (BCD). That was the maximum punishment that a Special Courts Martial could impose. SAC discipline frowned on acquittals so they didn't make weak cases. They assumed that any "pardoned" offender would sin again and receive justice. My previous case was the prosecution of a hinky Airman First Class aircraft mechanic who had placed sugar into an aircraft fuel tank. The usual pilot of the aircraft had corrected him for failing to correct a potential malfunction. His BCD was swiftly imposed.

The NCOIC was convicted and we entered the penalty phase. I had only one argument that could possibly sway against the BCD and I passionately argued that his World War II combat service, including the death march, had created for the government a chit to the Sergeant which had never been cashed. Pursuant to true justice I requested that they, for the government, cash the chit and not impose the Bad Conduct Discharge. I noted in the eyes of the court members that this young Lieutenant had an uncommon and unexplained appreciation for the warriors who fought in World War II. My advocacy for this soldier was sincere and they were swayed to decide that just a reduction in rank would be the meet and right thing to do. The sergeant was grateful and I then suspected that it would be some time before I would be back on a farm. It would be about forty years.

We became close friends with the Emerys and frequently dined at their quarters on fresh lobster. We also became close friends with the Busers and bought a larger trailer adjacent to theirs. Our small backyards abutted and the Buser child, Joey, soon toddled with Leslie. A laundry opened in downtown Stephenville and the neighbor Lieutenants occasionally curried favor with the ladies by washing the diapers at the facility. During the waiting we played serious Scrabble. Other times the ladies gossiped or shared their misery at one trailer while the gentlemen, in the other trailer, played Scrabble and sipped chilled red wine. During the winter darkness began at about 3 p.m. and the wine was usually chilled by simply placing it in the entrance foyer. I sometimes wondered that Miss Sara did not share in my appreciation for these nature-provided freebies. Christmas trees were another example. A perfectly symmetrical spruce, with five boughs perfectly aligned at each level, could be dug out of snow and cut at any roadside. My searches usually required a deeper foray because I dearly loved to play in snow and the search allowed this without giving the appearance that I was young for my years.

Friday nights our crowd and many others attended happy hour at the Officers' Club as there was no other place to go.

Two glasses of wine cost the normal price of one and the free food table contained sufficient hors d'oeuvres to suffice for a meal. We were making $401.00 a month including the forty-one dollar housing allowance. We were at a survival level only because we had no medical or dental bills and commissary food was dirt cheap. Occasionally our crowd had a back door caribou barbecue and the O'Toole Lieutenant claimed never to have eaten anything better. He had never eaten anything barbecued. He felt that his Irish roots compelled him to sip only Irish whiskey. One sip and I knew that he had strange taste buds and that his stomach was lined with cast iron. On occasion a stateside USO show followed happy hour. We listened to and met Bob Hope as well as a New York City rock band named "Twist-A-Rama."

During an early evening in November, 1961 I noticed a Mounty drive by the trailer and park in the street about two trailers down. He got out of the vehicle and I knew him well enough to recognize that his bearing and demeanor indicated he was pursuing crime. I walked to his car and asked if he needed help. He instantly accepted and said that a peeping Tom located in an abandoned house adjacent to an occupied trailer had been peering through a bathroom window while the inhabitants bathed. Would I go to the back door while he covered the front door? I knew what my duty was, but, for the second time, I had no weapon. I hesitated but seemed to remember that it was a crime in Canada not to assist an officer in need so I dutifully assumed my position. I waited and finally shouted concerning the length of time it was taking him to enter the house. He replied that he was waiting for a weapon being sent from the station. I learned that Mounties do not carry weapons and are permitted such only in emergency circumstances. The offender had absconded and my arrest skills were still untested.

I noticed from time to time that Miss Sara did not pronounce the "fun" in the name of this island. It made little difference because she seldom called it by its true name. We later traveled to Ireland with Miss Florence and I wondered why Newfoundland was not named New Ireland since it is an island roughly the size of Ireland, also in the North Atlantic, its settlers were almost totally Irish or Scotch Irish, and its landscape was similarly beautiful. The only real difference was that the English had not cut all of Newfoundland's timber. I supposed that Miss Sara was still sure that if she wandered a little too far in the wrong direction, she would be swallowed by that bottomless abyss that is the end of the earth.

The trials continued almost weekly and I continued to learn and improve.

9

R&R for bride; Lieutenant becomes
Staff Judge Advocate

During January, 1962 Miss Sara developed full-blown cabin fever. She was five months pregnant and needed to thaw out in the middle of an orange grove and only one place would do. I flew with her on Military Air Transport Service (MATS) to McGuire AFB in New Jersey, loaded her and Leslie on a civilian aircraft for Florida and returned to Harmon. Four weeks later I hitched a ride on a tanker to Hunter AFB near Savannah, Georgia, and was picked up by the family and went home. Two weeks later we returned to Harmon and were met on the flight line by the Emerys. The Major told me that I would shortly become the Staff Judge Advocate of the 4081st Combat Support Group. I was at first elated, believing that the Major's imminent promotion to Lt. Colonel had fetched him a higher assignment. I was much saddened when I learned the real reason for my new assignment and suffered great pain for my friend and father-figure.

Major Emery had reviewed for the Wing Commander a Flying Evaluation Board (FEB) proceeding. FEBs were convened to determine whether a pilot or other crew member had fear of flying. The Major, having flown as a crew member, explained that such a fear was almost never admitted and the proof was almost always the subjective observations of fellow crew members. The crew members seldom reported the matter unless a consensus had developed that the fear could result in errors of judgment that would put them in harm's way. When the observations became testimony it sometimes lacked specificity and depended strongly on subtle symptoms which, for the most part, involved mannerisms, bearing and demeanor. Piloting involved extensive and hard training and its reward was hazard-duty pay which could be up to 15 to 20 percent of a pilot's income. FEBs existed to accord a fair hearing before disinterested senior pilots in order that the dispute might be fairly, and, hopefully, correctly resolved. A recommendation to terminate flying status had serious repercussions for the officer's career and ego.

My own experiences led me to understand how a fear of flying could develop. God created man without wings and the earth with gravity. The Wright brothers' creation and its use would therefore always result in man tempting fate. I had already been told by senior pilots that the real definition of flying was hours and hours of boredom punctuated by brief periods of pure panic. I had already survived two such panic periods and had used these experiences to avoid a third.

I had made my trip home from Lackland after legal/chaplin training on a four-engine turbo-prop aircraft. The trip included a plane change in Atlanta, and as we approached Atlanta we entered a violent thunderstorm. The updrafts and downdrafts were severe and most passengers threw up. The male child to my left emptied the contents of his stomach onto my lap. After deplaning I was told by a ground mechanic that he was glad we made it but that there had been bets we wouldn't.

The recent tanker trip to Hunter AFB to retrieve Miss Sara had included the assignment of a parachute and instructions on its use. Over the ocean and offshore from Boston, we were at 30,000 feet and the fuselage was suddenly and violently being heavily bombarded. I put on the chute and wondered if I had paid proper attention to the instructions on its use. The co-pilot was frantically leaving the cockpit, gazing at the engines through a window, and returning to the cockpit. I was sure we were under hostile fire but would soon learn that the props had been allowed to ice up and engagement of their de-icers had caused chunks of ice to impact the fuselage violently.

During one assignment as Summary Courts Martial I had been assigned to sit at a Distant Early Warning (DEW) radar site located at the northerly tip of Newfoundland. It was near St. Anthonys about 250 nautical miles north of Harmon. The DEW line encircled the globe near the Arctic Circle and contained many such sites whose responsibility was to be the first to locate and track hostile aircraft coming over the top of the world. The sites by latitude alone were almost always remote and consisted usually of only the radar, quarters and a mess hall. The tour at such a site was only for one very long year and it was considered the worst assignment that Air Defense Command (ADC) had to offer.

During cold weather the site was only accessible by aircraft equipped with skis to land on a nearby frozen lake. At the flight line I learned that my aircraft was a very small two-seater civilian aircraft hired by the Air Force. The pilot was a Newfoundlander and his affirmations to my questions were, "Yes, bye." He volunteered that he hoped the ice would be thick enough to land on. I inquired as to how one would learn such matters and was told, "A low-flying visual inspection, good judgment and the luck of the Irish." I thought the luck of the Irish was always bad and responded that I was wasting his time because the trial had been continued. I did not confess that the continuance had taken place within the last ten seconds.

I returned to the office and explained to the Judge (Emery) that the pilot was unsure of the ice thickness and the trip had been canceled. I hoped he would assume the cancellation was the decision of the pilot. I was uneasy pondering whether not telling the whole truth was a sin. I was somewhat comforted knowing that I would disclose the whole truth upon inquiry. The Judge said only that I should have the NCOIC prepare a new assignment with a new trial date. The luck of the Irish was not always bad.

Major Emery's written review on legal sufficiency included a sentence that his opinion might not carry great weight because the Wing Commander had given some indications that his mind might already be made up. It was a mistake and it was within the "don'ts" that I learned at the knee of Sergeant Jesse Dinkins. Conceding my short experience in military affairs, I concluded that the punishment should be a verbal trip to the woodshed and not more than a letter, in the form of a written reprimand, which would be copied to his personnel file. The letter should also note his unblemished and exemplary prior service.

Instead, the Major was being relieved of duties as Staff Judge Advocate and temporarily assigned as an "Assistant" to the Base Commander. The order in pertinent part read as follows:

1. The duty assignment of MAJOR OSCAR H EMERY JR., 48743A, Hq, 4081 Combat Support Group, SAC, this station, is changed from Staff Judge Advocate to Special Assistant to the Base Commander. DAFSC is changed from 8816 to 7011 effective 29 Mar 62. Authority: AF Form 994A Card from Hq SAC, 21 Mar 62. FAC changed from 48000 to 01000.

 2. The duty assignment of 1STLT STEPHEN L
BOYLES, A03104408, Hq, 4081 Combat Support Group,
SAC, this station, is changed from Assistant Staff Judge
Advocate to Staff Judge Advocate. No change in DAFSC
or FAC. Effective 29 Mar 62.

Major Emery as an assistant had no specific duties. He
surely knew that his next permanent assignment would be
outside his beloved SAC. I knew that his goal had been to be
Staff Judge Advocate of the United States Air Force and he
now knew that it would never be. He had the right stuff to be
in that position. I learned that life wasn't always fair.

I silently wept when Major Emery explained that the mistake was his and that he would take whatever came. I knew
that he would take whatever came without whining. I was in
awe because I was in the presence of a great warrior. I noted
to myself that he was surely of Irish ancestry because he had
stoically accepted bad fate without complaining. My career
would forever be in his debt and I still think of him often.
After I was elected State Attorney of the Seventh Judicial
Circuit, the Emerys flew from California to specially acknowl-
edge the success of his best Lieutenant. We took them to
"happy hour," an event I shall later describe.

I was somewhat surprised when he suggested that, if inclined, I might do well in the Air Force. He explained that his
generation of Air Force lawyers would be retiring rapidly and
that the great majority of graduates of the Legal/Chaplain
School would put in their time and return to civilian life. Very
few had a bent for military life. This would, he said, create
grave shortages in the upper ranks and upper rank positions. I
privately knew from our NCOIC (NCOIC's are the only ones
who know all) that I had received the best officer performance
report that the Major had ever written on a junior officer un-

der his supervision. I suspected there was an understanding that the NCOIC reveal this but only after the Major had rotated. The Major's recruitment of the Lieutenant and his growing affection for the Citra boy required that he tell it now. He revealed that in sixteen years or so the Staff Judge Advocate of the Air Force would probably come from my class and that from his observations of other direct appointees I doubtless graduated at the top. I was dumbfounded that a man recently kicked in the butt by the Air Force was still an ardent recruiter. I instantly reconsidered and knew that he still loved the military and his recruitment duty was a duty to his country. This guy *was* hot s__t and I felt like cold cow dung. When I became Staff Judge Advocate his office was left vacant. His office, for me, was a riderless horse.

I knew that my bride had or would receive a similar version of these matters from Mrs. Emery. She would have to be prepared to quash the hot s__t warrior thing but she was seriously concerned. She suspected that the flag lowering and bugle listening had additional reason to intensify. Surely the son of Lloyd was bright enough to realize that what had happened to the Major could happen to him but he still had not sense enough to realize that his stubborn entry into the Air Force was a serious blunder.

The night would soon come when we would dine, for the last time, on fresh lobster with the Emerys. Miss Sara urgently hoped there would be no recruiting in her presence as that would require her to express opinions about career military service that might hurt the Major's feelings. She was in such pain that she, like Scarlett in *Gone With the Wind*, would have to tend to this on another day. I had learned that when pushed she became a true steel magnolia.

Recruitment was not mentioned during the sad lobsterfest.

No mention was made of the events leading to this parting of truly good friends. As they walked us to our car there were hugs and a shoulder pat. Mrs. Emery returned to her quarters and Miss Sara sat in the car. The Major and I shook hands; there were no more words. I came to full attention and saluted. The Major returned the salute, did an about-face and returned to his quarters. The Major never knew that when his back was turned I again came to attention and held a salute until he entered his quarters. My on-site, greatest generation "father" had stepped out of my life. I wondered if I could go it alone and get it right.

10

A rowdy lieutenant assaults
Base Commander

During Miss Sara's vacation in Florida I had been lonely and often had supper at the Club. One evening I was eating while at the nearby bar a group of rowdy lieutenants and captains were escaping their boredom by drinking beer. They were obviously just off alert duty status because they were in flight clothes. Entertaining themselves included the ritual that when one finished a beer they sang a short song and the man with the empty bottle threw it over the bar. The Base Commander was in a private room, in civilian clothes, and his party was being dutifully attended to by the Club Officer, a Captain from "All-benny" (Albany), Georgia. The bartender summoned the Club Officer to attend to the disorderlies but the Club Officer's instructions were ignored and the great fun continued. They got louder and the Base Commander demanded an answer from the Club Officer concerning what was going on out there. The Club Officer told it all.

The Base Commander approached the bar as a Lieutenant was throwing a beer bottle over the bar. He became the bull's eye on the Base Commander's target. The Base Commander was about six feet two inches tall, weighed about two hundred thirty pounds and had made full Colonel before he was forty years of age. He addressed the offending Lieutenant, informed him that he was the Base Commander and ordered that the revelry cease. The Lieutenant's reply would affect his career. The reply was that the Colonel didn't look like a Base Commander, he looked like a big fat SOB and, as the Lieutenant was replying, he grabbed the Colonel's coat lapels and gave him a vigorous shaking. Some of the Lieutenant's companions were sober enough to realize that this had gone too far even if the fellow was not the Base Commander. They restrained the offending Lieutenant not knowing the Air Police would soon arrive.

The Air Police arrived and started to escort the Lieutenant to the guardhouse to sober up. Pretrial confinement of an arrested officer was not common as they were officers and gentlemen until proven otherwise. The Base Commander, perhaps unwisely, continued to assist in removing the Lieutenant from the Club. During the trek down the hall the Lieutenant again assaulted the Commander and for the second time told him what he looked like. His trial brought many spectators and enhanced my education.

After escorting Miss Sara back to Newfoundland I learned from Major Emery that the rowdy Lieutenant had requested me for defense counsel. That created a problem because I already knew that I would shortly be Staff Judge Advocate and would be in the chain of command reporting to the victim of this crime. On the other hand a denial of available counsel might well have provided grounds for an appeal in the event of a conviction. Further complicating matters was that our NCOIC had revealed that word on the street was that the Wing Commander considered the matter to be one of "flyboys will be flyboys" when on a remote assignment. Punishment was necessary but it need not be severe. This was the same Wing Commander who had imposed great sanctions on Major Emery for his (probably only) lapse in judgment. I knew that the victim did not share the Wing Commander's view. He was sorely pi__ed off.

I was thinking that my farm training would be more important than my legal training in this matter. This journey would be through a cow pasture consisting of many piles of fresh ethical and political cow patties. It would require deft stepping not to soil my boots.

These circumstances caused me to remember that, early on, the Major had convinced the Base Commander to appoint me as the "permanent" Summary Courts Martial. Summary Courts Martial are usually done on a rotation basis by non-legal senior officers with much time in grade. The Summary Court was similar to the civilian Justice of the Peace. They had jurisdiction to deal summarily with minor offenses committed by Staff Sergeants and below. Their sentencing jurisdiction included the power to reduce a Staff Sergeant by one stripe, remove all stripes from an airman, and impose additional monetary sanctions in either case. This was the jurisdiction between "company punishment" imposed by the Company Commander pursuant to Article 15 of the Code and punishment imposed by a Special Courts Martial.

I performed my duties well but had, on one occasion, acquitted because the case had not been made. Major Emery had indicated the Base Commander would not like it but he would have to abide. I was not, as expected, terminated as Summary Court but I wondered if the Base Commander thought that I was "soft on crime." He did not know that I was the son of Corinne now burdened by concepts of due process. Life, liberty and property even in the Air Force could only be deprived when due process had been granted and due process required that the Magistrate be fair and impartial and that he render an acquittal when he had reasonable doubt of guilt.

The relationship of the new Staff Judge Advocate, the new assistant to the Base Commander (Major Emery), and the Base Commander resulted in a fair compromise for all concerned. After the Article 32 inquiry (a senior officer one-man grand jury) referral was made to Lt. General Sweeny (the General Court Martial convening authority) and the referral included some recommendations. The recommendations were made to Colonel Rydstrom (SJA, Eighth Air Force) by the new assistant to the Base Commander. The pertinent ones included that members of the court not be drawn from Harmon-based personnel and that the requested counsel (SLB) be co-counsel to a lead counsel who would be greatly senior to me in rank and experience. Co-counsel was normally referred to as second chair. General Sweeny complied. The Staff Judge Advocate of the 4082nd Combat Support Group located at Goose Bay, Labrador was made trial counsel and Major Murphy (from Massachusetts), an assistant Staff Judge Advocate to Colonel Rydstrom, was made lead defense counsel.

I began my telephone conversations with Major Murphy and learned that the only feasible defense to the more serious charges was probably intoxication. This defense was not available to disorderly conduct by an officer and gentleman. The serious charges included an element of intent and all elements had to be proved to support a conviction. Enough intoxication, under the code, could negate the ability to form intent. I was to interview the closest witnesses to the scene, the arresting officers and guardhouse personnel to get a better handle on its strength as a defense. I did some other routine pretrial preparation but my labors in this case were about over. My participation in the trial would barely be more than bringing

Major Murphy coffee during breaks.

Court was convened. I was about to have the educational benefit of watching two masterful trial lawyers. I observed that the Law Officer (the Judge in a General Courts Martial) had a look that he was also learning while watching these courtroom warriors. I reluctantly concluded that I was at best the fourth best lawyer in the Air Force. I wondered how many of this caliber were in the Air Force. I had some improving to do. In later years as State Attorney (SA) in a circuit which included over five hundred lawyers I would only see four or five trial lawyers as capable as these two.

Much later, on special assignment by the Governor, I would be prosecuting a Judge in Miami who was being defended by one with such skill and talents. He later became Chief Justice of the Florida Supreme Court.

Like most, this case was really about sentence. The prosecution put on its case and Major Murphy put on our case. Major Murphy was the best education I ever had in being a trial lawyer. When he was seated, his feet, flat on the floor, were at parade rest distance and he was erect but not stiff. Standing, he was never less than a perfect parade rest. Parade rest included being erect with the feet spread so that the outside of the shoe was plumb with the outside of the shoulder; the hands were to the rear, the left hand clasping the right hand, and they rested at the top of the buttocks. When at the podium he was at an easy attention with the hands placed gently on the front corners of the podium. His uniform, as expected, was immaculate and included the four-in-hand knot with the dimple.

The Lieutenant was convicted. The sentencing phase began and when it was his time the lead defense counsel went to the podium. He was spell-binding and centered on but did not mention by name three concepts. They were: he who has not sinned throw the first stone; how many are there, at least among males, who have not shown their butts when over-imbibing; and there but for the grace of God go I. It was done in such a way that the court members knew that he was talking about other sinners, not the court members. An artist had painted a beautiful portrait of mercy.

The court shortly imposed a sentence of reprimand and forfeiture of $150 per month for six months. I examined the lead counsel's eyes and knew he thought it was a win and if he thought so I had to concur. I briefly talked with the defendant and he was disappointed and wanted to appeal. I suggested that he find a new lawyer.

Miss Sara and I invited all the lawyers to dinner at the Club. All accepted except Major Murphy, who allowed he had found a chamber music partner and would be playing the cello. I amused myself by thinking that our common Anglo-Saxon roots might have had a mutated gene or two. We dined twenty feet from the scene of the crime but did not throw beer bottles over the bar.

During the dinner conversations the Trial Counsel stationed at Goose Bay allowed that Goose Bay was the end of the world. There was no off-base other than woods and tundra and access to the base was limited to air and water. There were no off-base roads. The weather, being continental, was much more severe than on the Rock. We, on the other hand, had a nearby town, roads, relatively mild weather and even a nine-hole golf course. I observed Miss Sara for some sign of relief that the abyss was over three hundred miles north-west and that her sorry lot was much better than many others. There was no sign and I suspected she thought the Major's prattling was at my request. His assertion that we lived in the "banana land" of Canada did not amuse the Brenau graduate. Miss Sara had no time for amusement. She had been a spectator at the trial and her observation indicated that Lt. SLB thought he had found his place in life. The wannabe warrior problem had been kicked up a notch. It had to be knocked down but she would deal with it after the pleasures of the next childbirth.

In fairness to Miss Sara's view of Newfoundland weather I need to confess that in the upcoming winter (1962-63) we experienced a severe blizzard locally called a whiteout. Whiteouts occur when wind and snow, in great volume, produce for the human being a swirling envelope of snow that reduces sense of direction to zero. I was at the Officer's Club for lunch when it began and remained there until it ceased, about nine hours later. There was, of course, no vehicular travel after the storm and as I walked home there was no snow or wind and an almost full moon. About halfway home I noticed a large "cone" in the snow--it was about ten feet in diameter at the rim, about twelve feet deep and the bottom was about two feet in diameter. I stood on the rim and observed a small portion of a vehicle's roof and front windshield. My vehicle at the club was by contrast only buried to a depth of five feet. This one, and many others , was buried to a depth of about seventeen feet.

Knowing that it would surely emphasize (in later years) Miss Sara's version of Newfoundland weather I nonetheless proceeded home and insisted that she and the children go and view the scene. They did and she conceded (with the stillness and the moonlight) that it was eerily beautiful. The remainder of her remarks were not learned at Brenau.

11

New SJA takes charge

The day after the trial of the inebriated Lieutenant I spent the entire morning closeted with my NCOIC. I had to learn the art of writing Officer Performance Reports (OPRs) and learned that I would also author his Airman Performance Report (APR). I needed to know how the records for review on cases that had to be reviewed by Eighth Air Force were compiled and the time limits to get them there. I asked if there was a rotation list for assigning qualified officers to Special Courts Martial. The Sergeant respectfully indicated that the Judge had pretty much left such matters under his superintendence. I rapidly corrected the mistake by asserting that he had taken a load off my shoulders and that I would follow the Judge's lead. I had forgotten some of Jesse Dinkins' teachings. My first lesson in administration was taught by a Technical Sergeant: Do not over-manage.

The NCOIC knew me well but he had known me primarily as a trial lawyer. He didn't know whether he knew me well enough to disclose immediately the source of my immediate administrative problems. He decided that this moment was the best time if he could conjure up the right words. He explained that we were getting mostly single direct-appointee Lieutenants who stayed only eighteen months and knew nothing about the military and less about trying a case. He knew that my time in grade would count for naught with them since they were not military minded and would not understand that I was the boss.

He need not have been concerned. Major Emery and I had discussed these matters at some length and I was prepared. He (the NCOIC), the NCOIC for the Base Deputy Commander for Security and Law Enforcement and I would essentially direct the administration of the Uniform Code of Military Justice.

The administrative problem was rapidly exposed. About 4 a.m. one morning I was called by the officer in charge of protocol. A Lieutenant under my supervision was the duty Protocol Officer and, after being called, he failed to meet the aircraft of a Lt. General. I called the Club Officer to stand by as we might have a Lt. General wanting an early breakfast. I drove to the flight line and personally attended to the pending protocol matters. I had a pleasant breakfast with the General and his aide and was much impressed that such a warrior was interested in my "story." The General was refueling and was on his way to assume command of Thule AFB in Greenland. He concurred that I would "handle" the absence of the protocol Lieutenant.

I contacted the Officer of the Day (OD) and requested that he go to the BOQ and deliver to the offending Lieutenant the message that the Staff Judge Advocate was at base headquarters and wanted him to report in dress uniform within twenty minutes. It was about 6 a.m. The Lieutenant reported sleepy-eyed but appeared healthy. I asked why he had not lawfully reported to his duty station and he responded that he was really not feeling well and added that this protocol thing was of questionable necessity. I, in a very serious tone, explained that whether he liked it or not I was his superior officer and he would follow my orders. I explained that the warrior he had missed meeting had a chest full of medals indicating that he had often been under hostile enemy fire and had survived a living hell. I doubted that the warrior "liked" being there. I further explained that the next time this circumstance occurred I would leave the flight line and visit the hospital emergency room and if he was not in the hospital and had not checked into the emergency room he would be in a different courtroom chair answering to charges of malingering.

His look told me that he would have to open the manual to find out what malingering was. Being the apple of the Emery eye could have been accomplished with much less effort.

There were no more protocol duty violations and I sensed the Lieutenants making some effort to shape up. They had now learned that not even a Lawyer Lieutenant is above the Code and all now knew that not obeying the lawful order of a superior officer was a crime. They also knew that the protocol duty offender was convinced that this slightly demented country lawyer would act on his promise. The NCOIC was making an extra effort to see that our work reviewed by the Eighth Air Force was "jam-up and jelly-tight." I often talked with Colonel Rydstrom, a man who often talked with a Lieutenant General, and concluded that Airman Basic Boyles had come a long way in less than two years. The Lieutenant General was Commander of Eighth Air Force and he, among other things, had flown the mission to drop the second atomic bomb on Japan. The office was beginning to operate as it should.

I was SJA only a short time when I received a call from the Wing Commander saying that the three-year-old daughter of a Captain had gone downstairs during the previous night and turned on the stove. A frying pan with grease ignited and caused a fire. The firefighters limited the burn damage to the kitchen but there was minor smoke damage to other areas of the on-base housing. He wanted to know if the Captain could be court-martialed. I indicated I would do some research and call him back.

SAC, to my knowledge, was the only command using the Management Control System (MCS). That system was designed to produce a Wing report card and it included many unannounced inspections. Quarters fires, vehicle accidents and bad checks were negative and weighty factors in compiling the report card.

I asked the NCOIC to get me the "complete" offending Captain's personnel file. The incomplete version would not include information obtained as a result of the security clearance inquiry. The file was that of a senior Captain about to make Major and with impeccable military and civilian backgrounds. He was, in fact, a tanker aircraft Commander with no hint of a fear of flying. He loved his job and had a very fine family. I was disturbed by the Wing Commander's call because the recent officer trial was done by the book to avoid even the hint that command influence was improperly playing a role in the military justice system. "By the book" included that preferring of charges (accusing) be made by a member's Squadron Commander. The Squadron Commander would often confer with the base SJA concerning the weight of the evidence and the correct UCMJ article under which to proceed. This informal review included consideration of the Air Police report of investigation. Preferring of charges against an officer always required an Article 32 proceeding. The proceedings in the last officer trial were slightly different because there had been an arrest based on obvious probable cause evidence that he had violated at least some Code Articles. The present case did not involve an arrest and did not involve any obvious probable cause. The convening authority, if any, would be General Sweeney and he would act after consulting with Colonel Rydstrom.

The Wing Commander was in charge of operations and the Base Commander was in charge of support which included military justice. The Wing Commander's role in military justice was only to set the tone of the overall strictness of code enforcement, and in SAC, that tone had already been universally set by General Curtis Lemay. It was generally referred to as "one strike and you get the bat up your butt."

There was a tale, generally undoubted, that the Commander of SAC had approached a flight line gate in a staff car with vehicle flags indicating that the gate guard was about to be in the presence of the greatest and most feared warrior then on active duty. The vehicle stopped and the airman, with an unusually precise and correct salute, approached the vehicle with stomach juices bubbling. The flight line badge was examined while really only observing the array of stars. The vehicle was waved on and stopped after only bare entry into the flight line. The General stepped rearward, approached the gate guard and returned his salute. The gate guard, standing at rigid attention with eyes straight ahead, had his stripes severed from his sleeves by the General with a pocket knife. He was then shown the General's flight line badge and saw that the badge photograph was that of a baboon.

The Wing Commander's role in the last officer trial had been only in the disclosure to his zebra-sleeve that "Flyboys will be flyboys." I believed that he believed this would result in other zebra-sleeves intimately revealing his thoughts to their Commanders and his tone would be set. The members, however, had not been selected from our base personnel.

I closeted with my NCOIC and wanted to know all the details, and *indicia* thereof, of command influence. I already knew that its most obvious manifestation was a convening authority improperly sharing his views on a case with a member of an upcoming court martial. That manifestation had resulted in unfair trials and, contrary to some civilian opinion, was then really quite rare. It was akin in civilian life to an accused or his prosecutor making contact with a juror who would sit on their case. The NCOIC obliged and told me everything he knew about the evolving administration of the UCMJ. It was an education.

I did my research and came to the conclusion that there was no evidence to support any charge. I properly called Colonel Rydstrom and informed him of the facts but withheld my conclusion. I knew that his staff would be put to researching the matter and I wondered if they would arrive at the same conclusion. I knew that Colonel Rydstrom and the ex-Eighth Air Force Inspector General (IG), Colonel Wilson (now our Wing Commander), were co-staff to General Sweeney and I was hoping he would volunteer information that would relieve the anxiety involved in my relationship with my Wing Commander. He only said that I should not return the call until I heard from him. I then knew that had there been a friendly relationship, *he* would have gotten my call.

A day or two later Colonel Rydstrom called and confirmed my conclusion. I called the Wing Commander and gave him the bad news believing that only my call to Colonel Rydstrom would secure my position as SJA of the 4081st Combat Support Group. I never really got close to the Wing Commander but I found during the Cuban crisis that, when in his assigned role, he was one super-fine and well-seasoned warrior.

His ribbons signified that he had distinguished wartime combat service and slowly I realized that during WWII Commanders had far greater powers of direct discipline than were permitted under the relatively new UCMJ. Under the Code, at least in peacetime, life, liberty and property could be deprived only after due process was accorded. The Code did allow limited deprivation of liberty and property under the Article 15 company punishment. It was the due process thing that was keeping my Wing Commander from efficiently getting the job done. The quarters fire had marked down his MCS scorecard and he was frustrated that he could do nothing to deter similar future transgressions. He didn't really like the MCS game but to make General he had to play and play well. I had the strange notion that I was balancing power under the Constitution of the United States of America. I had some doubt that my limited experience would be sufficient to get me a passing grade as SJA.

My better understanding of my Wing Commander allowed me to better focus on where he was coming from and, at least in matters of military justice, make sure that his direction did not lead him over a cliff. My confidence returned and I began to like and not fear my Wing Commander though I was still unable to forgive his treatment of Major Emery. I left for another day a plan that would let me educate him on command influence. I heard later that his new assignment would be Command College in Washington where they make Generals. Much later I learned that he had made Lieutenant General. I immodestly wondered if I shared in the credit for his career because of my tutoring him in military justice matters.

12

Twist-A-Rama: SJA the 'Ambassador'

The Twist-A-Rama (TAR) incident happened after I became Staff Judge Advocate. Twist-A-Rama required that I call upon my political science education to help solve a problem that was legal, jurisdictional and political. The incident tested the metal of my sword and would not be my last endeavor in such matters. Later, as State Attorney of the Seventh Judicial Circuit of Florida, I would be intimately involved with a case that involved a bounty hunter "kidnap" of a man who had jumped bail and fled to Canada to avoid land fraud prosecution under my jurisdiction. That tale will come later but it was said to have "strained" Canadian and Amer-ican relations.

Back to Twist-A-Rama. I do not recall the exact time of the incident but it was after March of 1962. TAR was a rock band and its club performance had occurred after happy hour on a Friday evening. On the following Saturday morning, very early, the base commander called me at home and said that his office was receiving calls from New York Congressmen asking why the American citizens who made up the Twist-A-Rama band had been plucked from the soil of an American AFB and imprisoned in a Newfoundland bastille. I dressed and proceeded to the office. The manure had hit the fan. Before leaving, I called the NCOIC for the Base Deputy Commander for Security and Law Enforcement and asked that he meet me in my office. I suspected from the brief conversation that this was his first knowledge of the incident. That was strange because he was a Chief Master Sergeant (three stripes and five rockers usually referred to as a zebra-sleeve) and his daily duties were to oversee the operations of the Air Police and base security. I remembered his amusement at having to "unarrest" a not-dry-behind-the-ears Air Force lawyer who had gone on the flight line without a flight line badge.

Shortly after arriving at the base my Extended War Operations (EWO) supervisor ordered the beginning of my flight line duties even after being told that my flight line badge had not arrived. I was sitting in a pick-up truck with a staff sergeant driver dutifully observing the refueling. I walked to a nearby hangar, went to the restroom, and upon exit a Master Sergeant wanted to see my non-existent flight line badge. I stupidly replied, "I'm in a hurry to return to my duties". I walked to the truck and was surrounded by security personnel bearing live weapons. I was confined under guard to an office within the hangar until zebra-sleeve arrived. Paragraph fourteen of the incident report read as follows:

> "At approximately 1322 hours, 3 Nov 1960, M/Sgt Roberts B.R., 4081st CAMS was working in building #839, he noticed a 1/Lt Boyles had entered the building. Lt Boyles did not have a SAC Form 138. M/Sgt Roberts notified CSC, where a 7-High was initiated. Lt Boyles was apprehended by the MST on its arrival at building #839, and brought to CSC. Major Emery, Staff Judge Advocate was notified. Major Emery vouched for Lt Boyles. Lt Boyles was released in his own custody at this time."

When I arrived at the office the NCOIC already had the answers. We both knew but did not discuss that he should have been the first to know that civilians had been detained by Air Police for possession of marijuana. I, as Staff Judge Advocate, should properly have been the second to know. Actually, the mistake had given me some running room. The arrest of the TAR personnel by an Air Policeman on a leased base lying on Canadian soil created some truly complex jurisdictional issues. Some extensive research in a later case indicated that proper jurisdiction was probably with the U.S. District Court for the United States located in the area where the TAR personnel resided. Probably they should have been "confined" to quarters to await a U.S. Marshal. The issue was seemingly moot because the arresting Air Policeman had delivered the quartet, consisting of two twenties-age males and two twenties-age females, to the Mounties at the base front gate. I had often heard that "possession is nine-tenths of the law." That proved true; the possession was now an affair of state for the two state departments. That gave me no comfort because Members of Congress were pressing the Base Commander for answers and the Base Commander was expecting the young Lieutenant to rapidly provide some. I did experience comfort, not disclosed to the NCOIC, in the sure knowledge that but for the mistake I would have been standing at the base gate in the early morning hours exposing my ignorance. The arrest was for possession of cannabis.

I became an acting ambassador without the hint of portfolio. My Air Force duties did include the monitor of Newfoundland justice meted out to Air Force personnel for crimes committed off base and those duties brought me in frequent contact with the Mounties and the roving Magistrate who regularly held court in Stephenville Crossing. I called my deputy lawyers and sent them to the books but knew our library would not suffice to provide any clear answers. I went to the Mounty

station to visit with TAR. We needed to assure the Congressmen that they were not being mistreated and I found them a
bit smart-lipped and agitated. The Mounties would not provide cigarettes, lipstick or mascara. I obtained these items
and depleted my weekly pocket money. There were no thanks;
these were regarded as entitlements.

I spoke with the Mounty Sergeant in charge. His rank
protocol-wise was the equivalent of a Major in the Air Force
and we had become friends in the course of my monitoring
duties. He was listed at the Officers' Club as my guest and
that allowed him unlimited access. He lived nearby and his
only other access to a facility with like amenities was within
a hotel at Corner Brook. Corner Brook was fifty miles north
and accessed by an unpaved rocky road which would wear
out a shock absorber in about three summer trips. It was of
course smoother in the winter because of the snow but safe
speed then was in the ten to fifteen mile-an-hour range. It
was more than a small favor to him, it cost me nothing and I
had better access to a system that dealt with things like airmen goose-chasing. Maybe I had developed some ambassa-
dorial skills.

The Sergeant told me that the Magistrate had indicated
that bail was not likely but that at his upcoming sitting at
Stephenville Crossing I would be able to discuss the matter.
During pretrial the TAR group was housed at the pretrial section of Her Majesty's Penitentiary in Corner Brook. The Sergeant would attend to their being properly treated. He finally
allowed that the Magistrate might be feeling a little heat from
the powers-that-be in St. Johns (the capital) and should the
Americans wish to entertain a plea we might reach a solution
accommodating justice and mercy. St. Johns was located at
the southeastern tip of Newfoundland and was worlds away

from our location. I, of course, was not representing and could not represent the people who made up TAR. A recalcitrant group entered Mountie cars and were transported to Corner Brook. I reported to the Base Commander and learned that Colonel Rydstrom wanted a daily report. His staff would do some research.

The response came the next day. The family and family lawyers wanted to know what the Magistrate had in mind. The Mounty-in-Charge was able to arrange a much earlier visit to Stephenville Crossing and I, the Lt. Ambassador, explored the Magistrate's mind. The Magistrate did not conceal his worry well and I suspected that his superiors were rapidly coming to the conclusion that his jurisdiction was very, very shaky at best. The offer was simple. The TAR members, upon a guilty plea, would be placed on unsupervised probation for one year with only one condition: that they immediately leave Newfoundland and never return. It was simply a face-saver. I amused myself with the thought that returning to Newfoundland was probably not high on the New Yorkers' travel priorities.

The Mounty-in-Charge immediately drove to Corner Brook to assure that I had complete telephonic access to the band members and, after our discussions, that TAR have complete telephonic access to their families and family lawyers.

I reported to the Colonel, was waved in without a knock, entered and was motioned to a seat in a way that said no salute was necessary. I gave him my report and he walked me to the door. This Lieutenant had unusual access to the Base Commander — he was getting some uncommon heat.

I made the calls and carefully explained that it was my opinion that the Magistrate had no jurisdiction but that might take some time to determine. I explained that it was their decision, that I did not represent them and could not make a recommendation. Finally I disclosed that it was theoretically possible that he might accept the plea and not abide by the agreed sentence but that he had always been honest in our prior dealings. I called Colonel Rydstrom and made my report and he called back the next day to say the families and the defendants wanted to do the deal ASAP. Shortly thereafter I drove to the courthouse which contained a much undermaintained courtroom located upstairs over a feed store.

The transporting Mountie was the same one originally transporting TAR to Corner Brook. He stood about six feet five inches, weighed about two hundred fifty, was muscular and uncommonly agile for a man that size. We shook hands, he flicked a finger and the members of TAR rapidly disembarked from the car. They lined up military-like at his heels and he "marched" the small squad up the stairs and into the courtroom. There was not a hint of recalcitrance. I saw no bruises, scrapes or scars. This large Mountie, I assumed, was a man of gentle persuasion. The proceedings were rapidly concluded according to plan.

I then drove to the base and learned that TAR had attained military-dependency "status" and were authorized air travel provided by MATS. Two hours later they boarded a MATS aircraft and flew to McGuire AFB in New Jersey. I reported to the Base Commander. The Colonel seemed uneasy when he realized that he had patted his Staff Judge Advocate junior officer on the shoulder. I was not offended-- friends pat shoulders in the south. There would be life beyond Twist-A-Rama. The young Lieutenant would get an outstanding OPR from his Base Commander boss. The "Patton" like destiny feelings resurfaced with added vigor.

13

SLB Jr. born; new apartment; Cuban crisis

During my duties as Off-base Housing Officer I discovered the availability of a new two-bedroom apartment that had a living room, a kitchen/dining room and, compared to the trailer-house, was graciously spacious. The Busers had gone home so we sold our trailer and moved to the apartment. Our linear living was over. The Air Force provided complete ranch oak furniture, a washer, dryer and TV. Stephen Lewis Boyles, Jr., came from the hospital to these luxurious surroundings in May, 1962. It would later be said that he was an apple that had not fallen far from the tree. The apartment had a yard but no grass. The lack of grass was noticed for very few days in Newfoundland.

During the spring and summer of 1962, the best event was the birth of SLB, Jr. He and a beautiful Minorcan lady would later marry, produce a first-born son, and name him Lloyd. As he got to high-chair status SLB Jr. provided Miss Sara with the best entertainment she had had on this bleak island. Finishing or almost finishing supper his eyes rolled and his chin fell to his chest. Abruptly his head snapped back and he made a vain effort to stay awake and then the sequence repeated until sleep took over. Probably you had cabin fever when this was your greatest entertainment.

In June, 1962 I boarded a tanker to Hunter AFB enroute

to West Florida to be best man for the roommate who was best man in my wedding. It was snowing as I boarded the aircraft and upon meeting the pilot I related the de-icing event. He was probably offended but there was no prop icing on that trip. The groom was my best friend in college and later, while a Circuit Judge, he was killed in an aircraft crash. A huge high-rise bridge near his West Florida home was named after Clyde B. Wells to honor his public service. He served in the Korean "conflict" and rose to the rank of Master Sergeant in breathtaking time.

The wedding over, I returned home flying in a tanker from Hunter directly to Harmon. I wondered if it would snow in July. There was no snow until late August.

Fall brought the Cuban crisis and it became serious. I was now also a staff member to the Wing Commander and as such more privy to just *how* serious. I began to consider that my decision to enter the Air Force had possibly put my entire family in harm's way. The advancements in both Russian and American air power had erased the strategic advantages created by the two major oceans. All of the United States would be in harm's way but SAC bases would surely be Russia's first targets and we would be high on that priority list since we refueled the B52s that would be going over the top of the world to Russia. Early in October the Wing Commander held a staff conference with those in need to know (I was present for some reason) and declared that we were now on full alert status. He opined that things didn't look well for peace. I assumed my presence had something to do with an explanation of administration of the UCMJ under wartime conditions.

I returned home and related to Miss Sara all the non-classified news. I expected the worst and got the best possible reaction. As upset as she surely was she quietly countered my argument that she and the children return home. There were more SAC bases in Florida than in Newfoundland and they were much closer to Cuba. It made good sense but gave me little relief. For the first time we arrived at a true compromise. She would stand by the phone and if I called she would load the children and seek quarters as nearly as possible equidistant between Harmon and Gander AFB (located in north central Newfoundland). This would be about thirty miles north of Corner Brook on the northern peninsula. The steel magnolia in these circumstances began to exhibit qualities possessed by the Mother of the Twins.

The stubbornness of the Irish Catholic Commander in Chief, with the probably loosened four-in-hand, averted the crisis and we soon receded from full alert. I would not have to determine if I was up to speed in monitoring the loading of JP4 and gasoline into the proper tanks of the KC97 under wartime conditions. Things returned to normalcy for me and as normal as possible for Miss Sara, considering her present location which dictated her sorry lot in life.

In early October I was promoted to Captain and received a letter from Colonel Rydstrom. I was being seriously recruited. The text of the letter read as follows:

> I am pleased to see your name among those selected for promotion to Captain. This promotion recognizes the good work you have done for us and, I hope, presages a long and successful career in The Judge Advocate General's Department, United States Air Force.

During December my present position included an invite, required attendance, to the Commander's New Year's Day reception. Only heads of staff, base Deputy Commanders and the Vice Wing Commander would be present. It included a caribou barbecue, revelry and a receiving line to greet the

Wing Commander and his lady. Most of those in line were Lieutenant Colonels with a chest fully laden with medals. The Brenau graduate was at ease and actually the most poised and graceful lady in the group. In her eyes was an expression that her groom might not in fact be hot sh_t, but he was a great deal more than cold chopped liver.

Shortly the permanent replacement for Major Emery arrived. He was a Jewish Lt. Colonel about 5'9", weighed about 220 pounds, was portly and about fifty years of age. Unlike the last judge he was a recallee whose goal was to get in his twenty years and return to civilian practice with a retirement pay cushion.

I was about to have my athletic ego shattered. I was playing handball regularly and was the best handball player on the base. I had taken handball as one of my required athletic courses in college. The 6'5" starting center on the University of Florida basketball team never did better than 21 to 10 when playing with the frog hunter from Citra. I wrongly enjoyed his frustration and I soon learned that pride and a haughty spirit indeed do goeth before a fall.

The portly LTC with the ample tummy and a bearing that included apparent laziness expressed an interest in playing handball. We went that afternoon only because he was the boss. I liked playing but I also played for the strenuous exercise and I knew beating the LTC would require little. I lost the first game 21 to 6 and my opponent, playing lazily, only strayed from a small area in center court to serve. On the other hand I strenuously chased balls, with six successes, over every inch of the court. Many balls I had no chance at chasing because when they left his hand they traveled a level plane, hit the back wall about three inches off the floor and skipped to the crevice between the side wall and floor. I never did better than 21 to 10. I knew I had been had when my opponent said that he left Barksdale AFB as the reigning champion. Barksdale had probably four or five times the numbers of our personnel which included some young and gifted athletes.

The next day the LTC adorned his walls with nearly a hundred handball trophies. I called Colonel Rydstrom to inquire how soon I would know about my new assignment. He informed me that with my enlisted service my time left would probably be too short to merit two household moves and that my obligation would be fulfilled in a non-active duty status if I did not stay. Miss Sara would have a husband who could tote groceries by October. I explained that I was still considering a military career but was having a hard sell with my bride. On a hunch I indicated that I could serve at least another year provided it was at a Florida base and provided we could leave Harmon in the Spring rather than the Fall. I explained Miss Sara's unhappiness and indicated better surroundings might possibly render her more amenable to considering a military career.

Two or three days later the recruiting Colonel called and said the closest he could get me to Florida in that time frame would be Moody AFB near Valdosta, Georgia. Valdosta was about eighteen miles from the Florida line and only 140 miles from Crescent City. It was also only about four hours from the other twin. I took the offer home and left out the irrelevant nature of its origin. I added that if we accepted the offer we would be leaving in about sixty days. I saw a smile and got a hug. Did I know the Colonel well enough to call him at home? Had the lady secretly been studying protocol? The days of wine and roses, in a habitable environment, would soon return for her. For my part it had been a tremendous tour personally and professionally.

14

NFLD tour over; trip home; Moody AFB

Chuck, the doctor friend, had finished his eighteen-month tour and during mid-April we convoyed to Port Au Basque and boarded the William Carson. The weather was about the same as when we arrived but, notwithstanding, we proceeded to the deck to make a home movie. My beautiful bride wanted to preserve forever showing her backside to the cliffs of Newfoundland. The ceremony included a bubbly lady, in parka, holding high the bottle that contained the source of her bubbly state. There was a toast to everything.

On the trip to Sydney we were in thick ice floes and that often required backing to seek an alternate route. One alternate route resulted in being grounded for three hours (One month after our first trip, the William Carson had been locked in ice for almost two weeks. The passengers had to be helicoptered to shore.) We went deckside to see why no movement. The sight was not pretty. Within scant yards seal hunters were plying their trade and we saw bloody seals atop bloody snow which was, in turn, atop sufficiently thick ice to hold small aircraft. The plane that was to have carried me to the radar site was there providing cargo transport to men, seal furs and seal flippers. My mind turned to the Irish poem that included a line essentially saying, 'May you live to see the children of your children'. I wondered if this pilot would have that much luck. I did a home movie of the scene knowing that our word description would be doubted.

We arrived at North Sydney, said good-bye to Chuck and, because of the delay, decided on a motel in Pugwah, Nova Scotia. We had recently purchased the largest used vehicle we could find: a huge 1960 Plymouth station wagon. We were carrying Miss Florence in addition to the children and SLB Jr. was still in diapers. Loading and unloading the contents of the car took nearly an hour and had to be done sequentially.

The next morning we loaded and made the trip to Canadian customs located adjacent to Calais, Maine. It was about 7:00 p.m. and we were only yards from American soil when the customs agents conducted a two-hour search of the car and its contents and found only a crockery Chianti wine container. They were dismayed that it was empty, it having been a souvenir from our going-away party. I suspected that other Harmon personnel had tried to carry through more than their limit of duty-free beverages.

We proceeded as planned to Dow AFB near Bangor, Maine where a room in the VOQ Inn was one dollar. We were already behind schedule and blinding snow coupled with a wrong turn caused us to arrive at about 4:30 am. There was no room at the Inn and we traveled easterly toward West Buxton. Miss Sara traveled in the rear seat to attend to the children and she did not lie down until we left Dow. Miss Florence was still my co-pilot and coffee had been refueled at Dow. During daybreak we saw a cluster of small cabins with a sign indicating "Open". They only had wood stoves for heating but that bothered not Miss Sara. She was a weary traveler wanting only a bed. We unloaded and slept.

That afternoon we arrived at Miss Florence's West Buxton cottage and settled in for the night. The Havu family of friends came over and wanted to hear about the tour. Miss Sara seemed inclined to discuss other matters. Some of these friends would from time to time use our house as home base to tour Florida. "Maniacs" are very nice Anglo-Saxons and less dissimilar to the Citra variety than you would think. They are hard-working, honest and friendly but somewhat reserved around strangers.

The final leg home took two days and it went without incident. I saw in the rear view mirror a beautiful mother now at peace and doing what she had chosen to do. Miss Sara never worked outside the home but she thrived on the most difficult and important career in the world. She would later use her home to provide day care for some or all of nine perfect grandchildren. Her name would be changed to Meema. It was now time for SLB Jr. to be in the arms of Miss Corrine. It was a good fit.

The rear-view-mirror scene also revealed a woman who had acquired lifetime chits because of the needless entry into the Air Force and its attendant tour to near frozen Hell. The only tour she had in the work force was a two-week stint working as office help in a Crescent City woodworking shop. She had also aimlessly attended St. Johns River Junior College and these two events made her aware that her instincts focused on motherhood. Her spouse would have to provide for her material needs and wants. She was never to acquire a clear distinction between the two. Much later I would be seated on my screened porch trying to determine whether the approaching wedding of our third daughter, Corrine "Jr.," would require a bank loan. The lady with the chits sat down and, seriously concerned, announced that our grandchildren had no place to swim. The pool was completed two days before the November wedding (no swimming would take place until

Citra frog hunter
with his Daddy

Nelline and Lewis, 8 years old.

The twins dressed for Sunday School.

Daddy shortly before
going to war

The twins with Momma

1952 basketball captain   Best looking 1952

"Pa" at Pigue's fishing resort

Juvenile shinkicker

The froghunter receives
a law degree

The grownup shinkicker

The newlyweds

First quarters in Newfoundland

EHAFB, Newfoundland — "Banana Land of Canada"

The Ptarmigan Hunters

v

Captain at cliffside

The new State Attorney

Courtroom warrior is now almost deskbound

The Boyles children — our greatest asset

Above: Our crew, 1999.   Below: the Boyles family, 1999

April) because its ample deck was the necessary dance floor for the home reception. It was at a level one step below the screened porch. The lady spent chits freely knowing they were endless.

I also recalled our pre-marital discussions concerning our marital roles. She heartily agreed that I should be the sole bacon provider and she, as homemaker, would cook it. I joked, maybe, that I would be Tarzan — a kind and gentle Tarzan but a Tarzan no less — and that she would be Jane. There was a smile but no laugh. I would never soar through the trees on a grape vine. I would never ever refer to myself as head of the household because I knew it would bring great laughter.

During the post-Newfoundland leave delay en route we drove to Valdosta and rented a three-bedroom brick suburban home. It had a small yard but compared to the trailer house it appeared to have some mansion aspects. We finished our delay en route and moved in. Sally noted that the drive "home" was under three hours and I noted that her fear of the abyss had subsided.

I reported in to Moody and found a four-lawyer office with a Lt. Col. SJA. Moody was Air Training Command with less focus on discipline than SAC. That, coupled with the fact that most airmen lived off base where their misbehavior was under civilian jurisdiction produced for me a trial load equal to about fifteen percent of what I shouldered at Harmon. It became a recipe for boredom. I volunteered to become claims officer and spent a two-hour lunch hour playing handball in order to maintain my prescribed physical fitness level.

Shortly after arriving at the base I learned that I would soon be certified by the Judge Advocate General of the Air Force as a Law Officer. I called Colonel Rydstrom to thank him because I knew it was his work. He opined that, at twenty-eight, I was the youngest to achieve that status and that was only because of the remarkable experience I received at Harmon. I did not confess that I was semi-bored. As soon as I was certified I called all SJAs within 200 miles to let them know that I was a "have gavel will travel" kind of law officer. I would later become that kind of civilian judge.

As claims officer I handled a claim that gave me experience in the greed involved in civil law suits. A Vietnamese pilot in training was soloing for about the second time and had chosen to solo at about eighty feet over his girlfriend's house which was located in the country about forty miles north of the base. His altitude was lower than tall Georgia pines (A southern expression then existed that an inebriated person was "higher than a Georgia pine"). At his altitude and speed any mistake could be critical. He crashed and burned in a cotton field.

The cotton farmer's claim against the Air Force arrived and I reviewed it. The claim essentially alleged that he had lost forty acres of cotton and the forty acres was scorched earth and would never ever produce a bale of cotton. There were no photographs. No matter. I welcomed a relief from reviewing administrative discharges. I obtained a staff car and, with photographer, drove to the site. The small T-42 had descended steeply and rapidly. The only direct or indirect damage was limited to no more than half an acre. I returned to the base and approved the claim for a sum that was very, very paltry compared to the amount claimed. My approval was reviewed by higher authority and sustained.

The first Law Officer assignment was to Turner AFB located at Albany (Allbenny), Georgia. The case involved a homicide that occurred near the NCO club. Court came to order and when seated at the bench I was slightly elevated above the President of the Court who was Brigadier General Paul W. Tibbets, Jr. I had the notion that this warrior, the one who flew the B-29 that dropped the first atomic bomb on Japan, was at least curious about a system that required him to "look up" to a very young Captain. The feeling was mutual.

After the trial we shook hands; he addressed me as "Judge" and inquired as to how I got to be an Air Force Judge so quickly. He said most Air Force Judges he saw were a Major or above and at least forty years old. I briefly explained while suppressing the need to be at rigid attention during a casual conversation with this warrior. I lingered with him until I was assured that we would be outside together and, with head gear on, I would properly be able to salute this warrior hero. Salutes were not exchanged indoors unless actually reporting to a senior officer. I knew but could not prove that this encounter was a part of Col. Rydstrom's recruiting efforts. I did know that the court members and law officer were selected by Col. Rydstrom and ordered by Gen. Sweeny.

My military career slowly became a non-issue for several reasons, the most important of which was that the nomadic existence of the military officer would simply ruin Miss Sara's life.

I also realized that it would not be fair to the grandparents and it would handicap the grandchildren. Most people, as was I, were about forty before they learned that their parents were always right. Most people were only about four when they learned that their grandparents were always right. Grandparents are thus able to reinforce easily the discipline not instantly accepted from an administering parent. Being one step removed has advantages.

Mid-September brought a cool front to Valdosta not normally experienced in Crescent City until three or four weeks later. The cooler weather would likewise last a little longer in the spring. The Valdosta summer had finalized the need for my North Atlantic genes to be in the coolest place possible. My country roots had also been reawakened. Suburbia was not for us. The coolest country place in Florida would be in one of the small towns near the Georgia line. I interviewed in Quincy, Madison and Monticello. One law office was over a feed store and I noted how handy that would be.

I did not know that Miss Florence, Miss Mayme and Miss Kate, (the Cason lawyer), were good friends and that Miss Sara was directing a conspiracy. Miss Kate practiced in Palatka and was told of the Citra soldier's accomplishments in the North Atlantic. Did she know any law firm in Palatka that might need such a promising young lawyer? She did. Our last day on active duty was May 1, 1964.

We soon bought a river home equidistant between Palatka and Crescent City. I rode twelve and a half miles north to Miss Kate's law office and grandparent visitation was twelve and a half miles to the south. This generation had increased the miles for grandparent tutoring by ten and a half miles. Often, on weekends, I made the trip "home" by boat with one or both children. The trip was up the St. Johns river through Dunns Creek into Lake Crescent and south to Pigues Fishing Resort. It was doorstep to doorstep and provided a view of God's spectacular art work.

The law firm soon took the name of Walton & Boyles. Both partners were, of course, graduates of the University of Florida Law School. The file involving the Cason & Rawlings trial was available to read.

15

Walton & Boyles; part-time
Assistant State Attorney

Miss Kate at first glance appeared as a gently reared Southern lady but on second glance I suspected that I saw the bearing and heard the wisdom of a true jurist. Miss Sara had chosen my civilian mentor well. Miss Kate was Kate Walton Engelken and her late husband Fritz Engelken was a former director of the U.S. Mint. She lived in East Palatka on several river-front acres in a large one-story cedar home until her death in 1985. The spacious yard had many large live oaks and included the slow-flowing and majestic St. Johns River.

Miss Kate had no children but she had three sisters and many nieces and nephews. The house's only permanent occupants were Miss Kate and many befriended canine Humane Society candidates.

I learned that she was well spoken, extremely learned and experienced in law and very knowledgeable about numerous non-legal subjects. She would become a true friend of the family and I would learn how to practice law at her knee. I was then serving under the third strong-willed lady of my life. It would be a rich experience. Our extended families became so close that most people thought we were all blood kin.

I sensed that Miss Kate was well-off and that her practice

was more about professional pleasure than money. She had a general practice but it included the handling of very few criminal cases. I started practicing with her in May of 1964. She was the best teacher I ever had.

Two cases would exhibit her "doing unto others". We had a client who had been sued by Jim Walter Homes for removing a Jim Walter home from property under mortgage to Jim Walter. The mortgage was in arrears. We lost in the trial court and appealed the judgment. We also lost the appeal. I learned that we received no fee and actually paid the suit and appeal costs out of pocket.

The other example involved an elderly couple living in nearby rural Yelvington near the Florida East Coast (F.E.C.) railroad right of way. It was an area of open range which meant that a neighbor had to fence cows out rather than the owner having to fence them in. During a railroad strike, management misapplied a herbicide to the right-of-way grass and our clients' 13 cows, each with a name usually dictated by a grandchild, had eaten the grass and turned belly up. We sued and received a jury verdict and judgment for actual damages in the sum of fifteen hundred dollars and punitive damages in the sum of three thousand dollars. F.E.C. appealed and only the actual damages were sustained. We did not receive any fee and we paid the suit cost. Our "fee" was later paid in legal tender of two 50 lb. bags of succulent cabbage.

We did have paying clients. We were on monthly retainer by the sheriff, tax assessor and Wilson Cypress Company. Miss Kate's tutorship in property law had early-on resulted in my being certified to examine titles for title insurance companies. This was accomplished by examining all public records, usually in an abstract, to determine whether a seller had marketable record title. We were usually paid one per cent of the sale price. On one occasion I examined the title on a large tract in Flagler County that was to sell for three quarters of a million dollars. We were paid the princely sum of $7500.

During early February of 1966, I was appointed by the Governor to the position of Assistant State Attorney (ASA) for the Seventh Judicial Circuit of Florida. That position was part-time. My monthly salary was income to the office budget. I was on monthly salary and bonus.

Probably in 1966 the Tax Assessor was sued by a group of school teachers complaining essentially that his undervaluing of real property was resulting in insufficient tax dollars to support adequate local government services to citizens. The tax on real property was a multiple of millage and value and since the County Commission set millage they were joined in the suit and would be represented by a local lawyer, Jim Millican. We lost the suit and the Circuit Judge entered a mandatory injunction requiring that these constitutional officers get the tax roll within legal limits and that on a regular basis we report to him on the progress. He set the time and date for the first report.

All defendants wanted to appeal because the ruling would surely have statewide impact. We appealed after my research revealed that the Notice of Appeal would act as an automatic stay to enforcement of the injunction. The Circuit Judge had lost jurisdiction until the appeal was decided.

We began preparing the appellate briefs. Because of the stay we had taken the time for the first report to the Judge off our calendar. Shortly after the appointed time, Millican received a call from the Judge's secretary indicating that our failure to show and report would likely result in contempt and jail time. The County's lawyer came to our office and I heard him explain in excited tones that he needed to see the members of this law firm because we were all about to be jailed. We walked to the courthouse and entered the Judge's chambers. Millican was obviously concerned over whether this young whippersnapper had sound precedent for the automatic stay. I produced the Supreme Court of Florida precedent concerning the stay. The Judge read the case and his demeanor indicated that I was on sound ground. He reluctantly apologized explaining that he did not know the appeal had been taken. That was probably true because most stays on appeals in civil matters were within the discretion of the trial judge. I remembered the incident with my Wing Commander and then concluded that lawyering was akin to flying. It was hours and hours of work punctuated by brief periods of pure panic.

Later legislation would enact this 'just value' concept into law. Later I became State Attorney of the Seventh Judicial Circuit and in 1973 became full time in that position. Miss Kate later represented the tax assessor in a law suit concerning the implementation of the legislation. The law suit had state-wide effect on the issues. Miss Kate's lawyer opponent was an up and coming lawyer from Miami named Janet Reno. I still had frequent visits with Miss Kate and she opined that Ms. Reno was "...one damn fine hard-headed lawyer." I learned later that their warring in the courtroom was often followed by high tea (cocktails) on Miss Kate's porch. They became close friends. Later Ms. Reno became State Attorney of the Eleventh Circuit (Miami) and while we often disagreed on State Attorney matters we firmly agreed that "sipping" with Miss Kate on her porch was truly a life-enriching experience.

Miss Kate and I often worked "overtime" which was usually done on her porch. The porch permitted a splendid view of the St. Johns River. These hours included the eating of small biscuits made by Miss Kate's housekeeper and they rivaled those of Grandmother Nellie. The housekeeper had a problem and became the top priority in the office. She had kicked her husband out but he returned and approached her door in a threatening manner with threatening words. She fired a pistol in his direction and he fled but returned later. He was then killed by a bullet that had been fired several hours earlier. The slug that killed him had stuck in the barrel but was propelled by the second slug into the chest of the deceased. The housekeeper was charged with first degree murder and Miss Kate made her bond. Robin Gibson, Miss Kate's nephew, was a very promising civil lawyer in central Florida and he completed the defense team. This case occurred before I became Assistant State Attorney (ASA).

The defense team worked and conferred. The night before trial we were on her porch fine-tuning roles. I reluctantly allowed that my view of the self-defense theory indicated it had about a fifty-fifty chance of succeeding. We chewed on that revelation and agreed to defer any decision. We went to the courthouse and learned that Circuit Judge Howell W. Melton was the presiding judge. (Judge Melton later became a Federal District Judge). Judge Melton wanted to know if the matter could be resolved without trial by jury. Luck was on our side because the Assistant State Attorney would assume we had a weakness if we initiated such discussions. A plea of *nolo contendere* (no contest) was reached to the lesser included offense (LIO) of manslaughter and the judge signed off on a sentence that included only probation.

Miss Kate's total personality was adequately rounded out by her activities with her numerous nieces and nephews. She had seen an amphicar and had to have one. The amphicar was a convertible and traveled, street legal, over land or water. Probably she had the only one in North Florida. Hers was the only one I had ever seen. She and her law partner could often be seen with several nieces and nephews driving down a public boat ramp into the St. Johns River. Then, to the utter amazement of spectators, they traveled upstream or downstream at will. Most of the nephew/niece conversation was gleeful description of the surprise in the faces of the spectators.

16

Prosecutor becomes warrior against crime

As Assistant State Attorney my duties included making the "charge" decision in all Putnam County and all Flagler County felonies. My trial duties included the prosecution of all Putnam and Flagler felonies plus trial of one third of the Volusia County felonies. I was under the supervision of the then State Attorney Dan R. Warren. The staff was rounded out by another Assistant State Attorney in St. John's County, one more in Volusia, and about ten support personnel.

My first trial of a murder in the first degree case as an Assistant State Attorney took place in Palatka. I was supposed to be second chair but the State Attorney was called out of state. I had traded places with the Assistant State Attorney in the housekeeper case. This now-defense lawyer had a booming voice and delivered it with passion. The case was about a white man in his seventies being good friends with a black man in his fifties. On the day of the homicide the black man received five dollars from the white man and fetched a bucket of chicken to be eaten together. They ate the chicken together at a table in the yard and the white friend inquired about his change. The black friend responded that there was none. The now-defendant stepped inside his house and armed himself with a single barrel shotgun. He returned to his porch and literally blew the deceased out of the chair to writhe in the dirt. The defendant reloaded, approached, and at close range nearly blew the deceased's head off.

I put on the State's case and the defender put his client on the stand. On cross examination I inquired of the defendant, "If you did not intend to kill the deceased why did you, at close range, shoot him the second time in the head?" The response was simply, "I wouldn't let a dog suffer that way." He was convicted of murder in the second degree and the foreman of the jury asked the judge if the man had been examined for insanity. The defendant was later sentenced to a term in prison which would mandate that he die there.

During a tour to Deland to try my one-third of the Volusia caseload, I was assigned to try a case with the following evidence: an employee in a Deland truck stop had gone to a bar adjacent to the world's most famous "highway" beach. Leaving the bar he drove northerly on the beach and impacted two strolling sisters at each headlight with such force that they were thrown in the air and killed. He returned to the truck stop and parked the car. The direct evidence included eye witness testimony which, pre-trial at least, was available from both husbands. The State Attorney had tried the first case and as I remember, the eyewitness husband testimony of that deceased failed. I prosecuted the second case and the defender was an Assistant Public Defender who would become Public Defender when I became State Attorney. We would become lifelong friends. His name was Robert Miller.

The defendant was convicted but his rather persistent advocate found a new precedent and appealed. The case was reversed based on the recent precedent of *Ash v. U.S.* Ash was a U.S. Supreme Court case which overturned a state court conviction involving a defendant who had robbed several people at a poker game. The first prosecution involved one victim and the defendant had been acquitted. The second trial resulted in conviction and the Supreme Court held that the prosecution could have only one bite of the same apple.

During my 1966-1967 tours to Volusia I tried many cases with the then Public Defender Joseph A. Scarlett. We did some serious head butting in the courtroom but always left together for a beer. We would later be opponents in an election for State Attorney and remain good friends. Outside the courtroom he was a charming and well-mannered Southern gentleman in the old school fashion. Inside the courtroom he was a warrior.

Later in Bunnell, the county seat of Flagler County, we butted heads after I became State Attorney. I was prosecuting game violators for assaulting a wildlife officer and breaking his shoulder. Joe in closing argument allowed that if the jury convicted on the paltry evidence put on by this over-zealous prosecutor he would quit the profession and return to farming. The jury convicted and every encounter thereafter was attended by "...thought you were farming..."

During my tour as Assistant State Attorney a tightly organized and efficient burglary gang was operating in most counties of northeast Florida. The gang was headed by Billie Joe Crabb and included Billy Wilson and two brothers. Their *modus operandi* was usually nighttime entry of a grocery store through the roof; they provided the hole, descended into it, cracked and peeled the safe and took its contents back through the roof hole. They had the equipment to remove the safe through the hole and that was done when a particularly secure safe couldn't be opened in the closely allotted time. Billy Joe Crabb had been tried and acquitted 35 times in several counties. They were true experts in their trade.

During the burglaries Pa was called to a secluded area

north of Crescent City and found two peeled safes. Some left-over documents pin-pointed the grocery store and thus the time and date of the burglaries. They were all in Putnam County. I assigned Pa and a deputy sheriff/State Attorney investigator to the investigation not knowing that the iron was hot. The investigation led to an interview with one brother member of the Billy Joe Crabb gang. He was relieved that they had come. He had gotten to the point that he could not go grocery shopping for fear that he might leave a finger-print. Shopping while wearing gloves would create attention. He told it all and about 100 cases, including four or five in Putnam County, were about to be made. I conferred with the other State Attorneys involved and a deal was struck (lighter sentence) for the brother member who would now set about providing concrete corroborating evidence of his disclosures.

Billy Wilson was in jail awaiting trial in Bay County. I sent Pa (Miss Corinne rode along) to transport Billy Wilson to Palatka for trial in our cases. During the course of the trip he revealed that he had once lived between Cross Creek and Island Grove in a dysfunctional family. One of his fishing friends was the male twin of a close-knit family who owned and operated the local grocery store. He believed that had he been raised in such a family he would not now be in his present circumstance. Billy had been a try-out for Jody in the movie *The Yearling*. Billy learned that one of his partners in the Noel Moore watermelon episode was now his prosecutor but not to expect any slack.

Billy Wilson and I had a long chat about the simpler days and pleasures spent in the *Yearling* lands. He opined that had he received the old-fashioned whipping I had received over the watermelon his crime spree might have ended there. We shook hands and he later pled guilty and took his punishment. I was left to wonder if the plea was made so that an old friend would be spared a distasteful task. I hoped his life would get better. I never saw him again.

Billy Joe Crabb was tried, convicted and sentenced to several years in prison. I shortly received a letter indicating that my visiting him in prison would prove beneficial to the state. I went and found that he could provide information that would solve hundreds of cases in northeast Florida. The *quid pro quo* was that he would be a confidential source, would speak to no one but me and if his disclosures provided substantial assistance I would support his parole when his presumptive parole release date (PPRD) was set. We both knew that the information provided to other agencies would have to be carefully edited and only furnished when several other sources were possibilities. Otherwise he would be disclosed and surely be killed in prison.

The deal worked and he was paroled on his PPRD. To my knowledge he led a crime-free life until his death terminated a rather short life span. During the days between his parole and death I had a source concerning the activities of several "damned outlaws." I had already learned that some Billy Joe Crabb members would have to be terminated from membership in the gang because they would secretly pocket an uneven share of the night's proceeds and "damned thieves" could not be tolerated.

These are, of course, a few selected cases out of several hundred that I handled and/or tried. I never kept count but I know the wins well outnumbered the losses. The juries seemed to like my "style." At the end of my tour as an ASA I had just turned thirty-three. The fact that Miss Sara had still not conceded I was hot stuff did not keep me from believing it was so.

17

ASA gets elected State Attorney

The birth of Sara Allyson caused our quarters to become cramped. Leslie was in kindergarten and Stephen was not far behind. The only one available was in Palatka and the only parochial school was also there. Commuting for Miss Sara would soon become a real chore.

We found a large Victorian house built around 1880 located in San Mateo and San Mateo was less than half the distance of our river home to Palatka. The house would require substantial renovation but that done it would be very comfortable and be consistent with our taste for the traditional. The house sat on three acres which included about seventy citrus trees.

We sold the river home and "camped out" in Miss Kate's sister's home which was located about one eighth mile from the Victorian house. This home belonged to the mother and father of Robin Gibson. Two months later we moved in. Allyson was two months old. Later Allyson would obtain both a degree in economics and law from the University of Florida. The law degree was *cum laude*. She would marry Patrick Currie, her kindergarten sweetheart. They produced two sons, one named Ryan Patrick and one named Christopher Boyles.

In December, 1967 the State Attorney resigned to enter private practice. The Governor appointed a lawyer from

Daytona who would have to run in 1968 to keep the job. He was a fine, decent man and lawyer and also happened to be a Justice of the Peace. He later became a good friend. However, he had never prosecuted or defended a felony in court. My General Patton-like penchant for being able to read my own destiny kicked in. I wondered how it would be received by the one who had the chits to veto any more foolish career decisions. There was no immediate opposition, probably because my election if it improbably occurred would not require a household move or a separation from Miss Kate. The SA position was still part-time and civil law practice was allowed.

I discussed it with Pa and Miss Kate and few others. My political naivete became both a blessing and a curse. The curse was that I had not carefully examined my political chances. I would be 33 years of age during the campaign which would begin with the spring primaries in 1968. Only one other State Attorney in Florida had been elected at an earlier age and I appeared younger than he looked when he was elected at the age of twenty-eight. Volusia County had more than three times the population of the other three counties combined and, probably because of that, a non-Volusian had never been elected State Attorney of the circuit. I had no money to support such a campaign, didn't know what it would cost and realized that my nature would not well equip me for raising money from strangers. I did not know the political powers-that-be in each of the four counties but I suspected that their help would be at a price that I, as the son of Corrine, could not pay. I knew that outside the courtroom I was still a bit bashful and shy. I did not easily mingle or chat with strangers. The blessing was that had I analyzed such matters I probably would never have run.

I resigned my position in March, believing that it was not good for the office to have an Assistant State Attorney running against his boss. The ASA in Volusia became a candidate and did not resign. Friend Joe Scarlett became the final candidate in the Democratic primary and the State Attorney had no Republican opposition. I announced and the race was on. The only plan was to run some political ads and attend all political rallies which permitted a three-minute campaign speech. Mine was that my six-year experience in prosecution, four in the military and two as Assistant State Attorney, really amounted to about fifteen when you considered the number of cases handled.

I received a call from Edward L. Brooks wanting to know if he could help. I told him I would call back and asked Miss Sara, "Who the heck is Ed Brooks?" She had no answer. I did some inquiring and found that he was from West Virginia, married to Delores, and was a management employee at the local paper mill dealing with the shipment of paper. That was all I knew when I returned his call and told him that the first rally in Putnam County would occur shortly in Welaka. We agreed to meet there, we did, and in my speech to the crowd I forgot my wife's first name which proved uncommonly entertaining to many of my former high school classmates. Ed, referred to by Dolores as "Eddy Lee," and I agreed that he would compile a list of all rallies and we would attend them as a team. We would, together, draft all political ads we could afford and maybe rent some billboards.

Ed would later be elected Palatka City Commissioner, appointed Tax Assessor, elected for a second term as Tax Assessor, appointed Director of the *ad valorem* tax division of the Department of Revenue, Executive Director of the 7th Judicial Circuit State Attorney's Office and serve two elected terms as the Clerk of Court for Putnam County. These last two terms would be served with his shy candidate.

I, as the chief administrative judge for Putnam County, would much later have the high honor to proceed with Miss Sara to Orlando and swear in the new president of the Florida Clerks of Court Association. My remarks concerned how their Edward L. Brooks was really Eddy Lee and that he single-handedly engineered my first election to public office. My remarks centered on the campaign and they were made with my best sense of humor. They closed with a very serious personal and citizen appreciation and acknowledgment of his true friendship and true public service. The crowd was immediately transformed from belly laughs to tears. We would be told, and I would believe, that it was the best speech they had ever had at these annual gatherings. I suspected that I would soon be kicked in the shin.

Ed and I began. We attended all the rallies and, my Welaka nervousness over, I began to learn that experience at the courtroom podium was beneficial to performance at the political podium. We traveled the circuit, I made the campaign speeches, and he worked the crowd. We were getting volunteers who wanted to help and this family/friend campaign began to widen.

An old family friend who had been with Pa at Camp Blanding and only recently known to me as Brigadier General William M. Thames, Ret., then lived in Ormond Beach. He became involved. He and his Friday afternoon "happy hour" would later greatly expand my family of friends.

Pa had a nephew, Wallace Smiley who was married to Edna who was a member of the Crescent City Miller clan. The Millers ultimately became grocery store magnates. Wallace and Edna lived in Daytona and were both principals in Daytona area schools. Wallace, Edna and their young children Bruce and Joy became involved. Miss Florence had a deceased brother who was sheriff of Seminole County and had retired in New Smyrna. His descendants and her antique collecting friends in New Smyrna were recruited. A small pebble thrown in the water was creating some disproportionate waves. The powers-that-be and the political pundits, their ears to the political ground, had concluded that the boy from Citra had a remote chance to cross the line as place rather than show but he had no chance to win in the run-off.

They did not know that the country boy had inexplicably impressed Josephine Davidson, the New-York-bred daughter-in-law of the owner of the *Daytona Beach News Journal.* Ms. Davidson had also impressed me. There were five members on the editorial interview board, including the owner, but there was no doubt about who was in charge. Ms. Davidson was. This lady had a bearing and directness which indicated we were not there to chat, we were there for her to pierce the inflated *curriculum vitae* in order to determine whom they would endorse. I was not a good chatter and my answers were as concise and direct as her questions. Yes I was personally in favor of capital punishment but only in the mad-dog-killer cases. I explained that they could escape and continue the carnage or they could continue the carnage by killing other inmates or guards. I knew she was opposed but her eyes, not her next questions, indicated that she would at least have to rethink her position.

The last Saturday before the upcoming Tuesday primary found us at Deltona, about sixty-five miles south of Palatka, having a 7 a.m. coffee with a group of ladies who were being recruited by a lady who had made up her mind at an earlier rally. This had become not an uncommon occurrence. We, with the ladies, toured the shopping center while they handed out campaign cards to their neighbors. Did they want to meet their candidate? — he was right over there.

We drove north to Bunnell and had a one-hour layover in a lawyer supporter's office in order that the candidate could have a cat nap. The cat nap over, we drove to Moccasin Branch for the best-attended St. Johns County rally. Leaving Bunnell we noticed that the bicycle-age son of the manager of the local Ford dealer had a "Boyles for State Attorney" bumper sticker on the rear fender of his bicycle. The rally at Moccasin Branch included a feast on the then-legal gopher tortoise stew. We left there and returned to the pier at Daytona for the final organized rally.

This rally included a flourish with two young short-skirted ladies going to the spectator section to retrieve and escort each candidate to the podium. When my time came they went to Eddy Lee, several seats away, and he was heard to exclaim excitedly, "It is him, over there!". They finally came to my elbow and I had the windfall makings of some remarks they would enjoy and remember. My new NCOIC had outranked me in politics but volunteered to drive home.

We awakened on Sunday to learn that the *Daytona Beach News Journal* had endorsed the "wannabee" soldier in strong and glowing terms. I knew it was the pen of Ms. Davidson and I first realized that her following me to the door for the exit of the interview with a "good luck" was meant to relieve my anxiety. Not even the candidates were allowed to know the endorsement until it was published. Ms. Davidson and I would later become very good friends and uncommonly share views from divergent backgrounds. She would often call and inquire concerning my views on judicial candidates and at social gatherings she would allow that my civil duties as State

Attorney were on, or off, track. I would much later be a select invitee to an organization formed to honor and memorialize her accomplishments. I assumed the list of invitees came about from her discussions with her husband.

The following Tuesday was election day. The candidate without a chance was elected Democratic nominee without a run-off. He had more votes than the other two combined. The Crescent City vote was Boyles over two hundred and Scarlett and Masters shared about a dozen. Eddy Lee relaxed for the summer and I learned that he had top secret service clearance in intelligence matters as a NCOIC in Japan. He also had an assignment as bugler to play taps at Arlington military funerals. He had left Appalachia for the same reason many had left - to obtain a good job. He had married Delores, a co-worker at Hudson Paper company, after a brief courtship. Delores was reserved and shy. He, as he had demonstrated, was able to cause the election of an otherwise unelectable candidate.

The general election was easier. There were no partisan rallies and the civic rallies had tapered off. It was mostly door-to-door, shopping centers and shaking hands with people entering or leaving a shift change at a hospital or a facility like the Hudson Paper Mill. Ed and many of our newly-recruited campaigners thought I should make every shift change at every such facility employing more than 50 employees. I declined some as I still had duties to clients that had to be attended to. I won the election but lost slightly in St. Johns County. I compared my election results with other races such as U.S. Senator and President and learned that this circuit, and much of Florida, was becoming Republican in voting if not in registration. Twenty years later I found out that this trend had become fact.

18

Young SA gets the job done

My first four year term began January 7, 1969, and they were the "fun" years. I had the same small staff and the Governor had replaced my vacancy with a man named George Newton. I appointed Richard O. Watson of St. Augustine as an ASA in charge of St. Johns County. Dick had been a classmate in law school. George and I were in the same church and together hosted the church men's breakfast. He was a court reporter but studied law under J.V. Walton and Miss Kate and after "examination" by the Supreme Court of Florida had become the last member of the bar without a law degree. He had also become the last Assistant State Attorney to be appointed by a Governor. New Florida law would give that power to the State Attorney.

As an Assistant State Attorney I had recently prosecuted a barroom murder in Bunnell, the county seat of Flagler County. Mr. George was the court reporter and, as such, he sat about four feet from the witnesses. The case involved a barroom which was about fifteen feet by twenty-five feet. Several fights "broke out" including a vicious one between the defendant and the deceased and it included several beer bottle blows. When the deceased stepped out the front door the defendant shot him, the bullet landing squarely in the middle of his temple.

I called several witnesses to establish death, cause of death and identification of the deceased. I called my "star" witness, an eyewitness from the police reports, and asked if he would state for the record his name. He simply replied "Frogbelly." I asked for his Christian and surname and he replied, "That's it — Frogbelly." I was observing a court reporter having one hard time in "holding it." I had no real choice so I began with, "Mr. Frogbelly, were you at the bar on the date and time of the shooting and did anything unusual occur?" I saw again a court reporter almost "losing it." The answer was he was there but neither saw nor heard anything unusual because he was playing poker. I was recovering and knew that it would be pointless to ask if he ever spoke "any evil." I then recalled that I had recently prosecuted a murder in the same county which involved a poker game homicide over one dollar. Later Mr. George was known to introduce himself as "Frogbelly" and he would be greatly amused by the stares indicating that he must really be from a looney farm.

On January 6, 1969 my predecessor selected a jury for a first-degree murder trial that had commenced in Flagler County. The next day I was the State Attorney and became the prosecutor. Two hitchhiking outlaws had been picked up by two young boys driving a small sedan. They killed both boys; one was shot three times in the face and all wound entries were "contact," contact meaning the weapon touched flesh. Dr. Arthur Swartz, the medical examiner, indicated that contact facial shootings were really rare and they were always the work of very evil, wicked and twisted personalities.

The trial of Kit Hayden was first and it took about three days and was without unusual incident until the verdict was read. I noticed that there was no juror eye contact with the defendant when they exited the jury room and that usually meant a verdict of "guilty as charged." Eye contact with the defendant usually meant conviction of a lesser charge or an acquittal. My experience then allowed me a ninety percent correct guess as to which of those two had occurred. My eye contact with the defendant revealed the soul of a mad-dog killer whose "high" occurred only when killing. Surely Ms. Davidson would have to agree that this man deserved to die.

The verdict form included a number of lesser included offenses (LIO's) and one lesser was assault with intent to commit murder in the second degree. That was the verdict as read and all observers were stunned. The evidence had included the medical examiner testimony concerning the cause of death and full-face morgue photos showing the facial bullet entries. I was more than stunned because this verdict carried a maximum punishment of twenty years in prison. I did the only thing I could do and that was to request that the jury be polled. They were polled one by one and each juror responded "Yes" to the clerk's question, "Mr. _____, is the verdict as read your verdict?" I was thinking this had to be a colossal mistake and I knew that it probably could not be corrected after the jury's discharge which was imminent. I tried to buy time and went to the clerk and asked to see the verdict and noted that it had been correctly read. Hopefully the aghast look on my face would produce some juror response. It did not and the jury was discharged.

Judge Wm. E. Wadsworth sentenced Hayden to twenty years before we recessed. Shortly thereafter I was on the front steps having a conversation with the bailiff in charge of the jury. I knew that he was the likely one to have heard anything that would make the verdict understandable. He volunteered nothing but two jurors returned to the courthouse, walked up to me, and wanted to know why that "damned Wadsworth" had sentenced that mad-dog killer to only twenty years. I explained that was the maximum punishment for assault with intent to commit second degree murder. They responded that they convicted him of second degree murder. I asked the bailiff to inform the judge and defense lawyer and I hastened to the library. My worst fear was confirmed: these facts would not permit a correction. Discharged jurors leaving the courtroom are no longer under a mandate of not reading or hearing anything about the case except what they see or hear in the courtroom while the case is in trial. Thus once tainted they cannot redeliberate. Our justice is the best in the world but it was and is not perfect.

Judge Wadsworth and I tried about a dozen capital cases in Deland over the next ten or eleven months. Four of the cases involved a gang rape of a coed during the now-famous spring break at Daytona Beach. The coed and her date were lying at water's edge on a remote portion of the world's most famous beach. It was about 10 p.m. when a car carrying five male college students passed their location and then stopped. Four of the group exited the car, walked to the couple, and each raped her while the other three restrained her date. The fifth occupant only stood by the car and observed. The four made a huge mistake when they boasted of their "conquest" to a fellow student back at the dorm. He reported the matter to the police.

The trials had to be separate because some pre-trial incriminating admissions implicated not only the defendant on trial but other defendants as well. That was impermissible for the jury to hear. Strong possibilities existed that such oral admissions might also be blurted out by the interviewing police officer and that would be a mistrial. Redacting the impermissible portions of written admissions would likely confuse the jury.

I will deal with only the last trial. I put on the State's case but the fifth passenger witness was now in federal custody and he was brought into the courtroom by federal marshals. He was shackled and his credibility had weakened for other reasons since the other trials. The reporting witness had difficulty sorting out exactly who said what when they had reported their conquest. The victim had a "nervous" smile which obscured the severity of the horror she had endured. There were problems but I was still secure in the soundness of the case. I rested for the state.

The defense called only one witness. It was the defendant's mother and she lived about two and a half hours, by vehicle, south of Daytona Beach. She appeared credible and testified that her son was home on the day after the offense and defense counsel believed an alibi had possibly created reasonable doubt. The lady appeared truthful to me so I asked a simple question (violating the advocacy rule that you don't ask a question if you don't know the answer): "What time did you first see your son on that date?" It was at 3:30 p.m. when she returned home from work.

My rebuttal evidence consisted only of one police officer witness testifying about distances and driving times from the crime scene to her home. The normal drive at legal speed limits would be about three hours and from 11 p.m., about the termination time of the rape, until 3:30 p.m. the following day would provide ample time for the trip. The defense counsel was somber and wondered if he had properly given up closing argument. A defendant who puts on no evidence other than his or her own testimony gets opening and closing argument with the state having only the "middle" argument. The reverse was now true in this case and most trial attorneys believed the last word was very important.

The jury returned deadlocked or "hung" because they could not reach the required unanimous verdict. The judge gave them an instruction which said he could not order this but his request was that they deliberate further to see if the impasse could be resolved. A hung jury required a re-trial before a new jury. They returned still deadlocked and were discharged.

Four days later I received a letter from a female juror suggesting that this very guilty defendant deserved his due. She wrote that she was the only holdout for acquittal and that was because the defendant had more than adequate time to do the crime and drive home before his mother arrived! I was having some pain wondering how often true jury mistakes were made.

I am happy to note here that my future experiences would indicate that they occur far less than one percent of the time.

We by then (early seventies) had three beautiful, bright, talented and well-mannered children. We were entering the days of softball games and piano recitals. I was balancing my time between prosecution, practicing with Miss Kate and parenting. I slowly discovered that attending to all took more than forty hours per week.

I drew plans for renovating the house and they included the tear-down of the original one-story rear portion of the house and its replacement with a large two-story version that was much more compatible with the front portion's two-story lines and gables. The front portion had itself been an add-on to the original. A bonus occurred when I included the original floor joists and sills (from under the floor of the torn-down portion) as uprights and exposed ceiling joists in the kitchen, family room and side porch which later got the required adjacent pool. They were over 100 years old, were heart pine and had been hand hewn with a foot adz. Every new visitor would have eyes that immediately focused on their antiquity and beauty. No first visitor ever realized that this section of the house was about ninety years younger than the front section. It became a super large and super comfortable home. It would host many, many special events for large numbers of family and friends including wedding receptions for all the children.

19

After 10 years in the courtroom, a trip to Maine

The renovation began in 1970 and we were living in a mobile home temporarily placed in the back yard while the renovation was accomplished. It was summer and Miss Sara was pregnant with our fourth child. She had a learned aversion to living in a trailer while pregnant and I suspected she did not want to witness the actual unfolding mistake that would result from the works of the wannabee architect. My plans were drawn on a legal-size note pad with only pencil and ruler. Changes were sometimes drawn on a grocery bag. She wanted a vacation and I concurred. I had had few breaks from the courtroom over the past nine years.

Pa had recently been operated on for bladder cancer and that followed being shot while arresting a fugitive in an abandoned house. He was still ambulatory and active but my conversations with the doctor indicated that status would last only for a few months. If we were going we needed to go right away because I would soon be sorely needed by my mother and "father."

The Boyles, Brooks and Watsons (Dick and Peggy and two sons) boarded separate rented motorhomes and began a convoy to Maine. When leaving I, from the driver's seat, instructed the builder that it would be random width cedar in the kitchen/family room and the ceilings would be random width cypress. The porch ceiling would be pic wic pine. The ceilings would be nailed on top of the exposed ceiling joists and their top side would be the floor of an eighteen inch crawl space between floors for plumbing and electrical placement and access. The height of the ceilings would be dictated by the upper floors of the new and old sections of the house being on the same level and a required thirty inches to accommodate the crawl space and the twelve inch upstairs floor joists. I allowed that this would probably make the downstairs ceilings about nine feet four and one fourth inches in height. We left the yard and I was getting the hot shi_ look but I knew that the fear of the great mistake had partially subsided.

Miss Sara did better sleeping while riding pregnant even in a motor home. She was again not a totally happy camper. We left slightly before dark and traveled north but we were seeing few real camp grounds. We crossed the South Carolina line and saw a campground sign and turned in. It had no facilities other than picnic tables, was dark and was occupied only by a motorcycle gang sporting many tattoos. I slowed down only enough to accommodate safe driving. We had no communication devices between motor homes except sign language which was conveyed from our rear window to coach two, and, in turn, to coach three.

They did not know that we were headed to the backyard of first cousin once-removed Judson Rickenbaker in Round O, South Carolina. We arrived at daylight unannounced and were warmly greeted by Judson and his wife Marguerite. Marguerite graciously attended to all our needs while Judson roamed the neighborhood exclaiming to the Rickenbaker clan, "Come to our house, Lew-ese from Florida, Jeat's own, is here". My last visit had been several years ago to attend a funeral. Judson's back yard was quickly filled and the beginnings of a Southern feast were quickly under way. I disappeared and took a short nap before the noon feast which included home cured ham and home grown vegetables made into a stew served over rice. The Brooks and Watsons seemed a bit overwhelmed by such hospitality under such circumstances. In the early afternoon we left and I learned that Miss Sara could perfectly mimic the Geechie accent. I looked for and found a book listing locations and facilities of available campgrounds in the eastern United States.

I did not disclose, even to Miss Sara, that the visit with the Rickenbaker clan was not unplanned. My deepest roots in American soil were located in the farm country (and woods) between Round O and the Ogeechee river. It was slightly undulating and heavily timbered. It contained many small and well kept Baptist churches, always frame and clapboard. Most of those churches were isolated from other man-made structures and their grounds always included a covered table for "dinner on the grounds". I suspected the isolation was purposeful; that is, a closer commune with your Maker was furthered when you saw only what He had made. I have recently read professional dissertations indicating that isolating oneself in nature where there is no evidence of other mankind (and his works) will wipe out stress and anxiety. I had experienced that in Newfoundland.

Leaving Round O I recalled that on our last family reunion there we visited the family cemetery. We discovered two small headstones of male and female twins. They were Homer and Madge Rickenbaker and they were born December 30, 1905 and both died during August of 1906. They were my and Nelline's first cousins twice removed. You should recall that we were born December 30, 1934.

We traveled on, stopping at campgrounds and cooking on open fires. Between Washington, D.C. and Harrisburg, Pennsylvania we finally noticed that the Watson carriage was not in the rear-view mirror. We and the Brooks backtracked about 30 miles and saw the lost vehicle parked on the pull-off very close to a guard rail-- so close that the only permitted exit was through the driver-side window. R.O. had a battery failure and he was steaming. I cannot repeat his language.

We replaced the battery and spent the night at a campground in Fort Indiantown Gap, PA. Part of the campground included an antique, but operable, carousel. It was a delight for the kids. We traveled on and finally arrived at West Buxton. Florence and Mayme were there and settled in for the summer. We found a nearby campground and settled in for four days.

We explored Maine, visited with the Havus and occasionally dined on fresh lobster and steamed corn still in the husk.

We left Maine and traveled homeward. We toured Gettysburg. We spent one night at Bradley's campground near Hiawassee, Georgia. Hiawassee would become my home away from home and I would, with an old friend named Byron Butler, do some real estate developing including the construction and sale of three cabins.

We spent the next night at a Stone Mountain campground and my twin and her crew joined us around the campfire. Sometime later during the Butler-Boyles cabin building Nelline and Roy became interested in Hiawassee. They ultimately retired and moved there as "permanents."

We returned home and the addition had a roof and the "100"-year-old fireplace was completed. Everything had been done according to plan and I noted that Miss Sara was well pleased. Her final trailer days were over.

20

Pa's death

Pa was rapidly deteriorating and had to be hospitalized frequently at Halifax Hospital in Daytona Beach. The hospital was near my State Attorney headquarters. Mama stayed with him during the day and spent the night with the General's sister-in-law, Miss Vera. I worked days and took the night shift with Pa. He was then receiving blood transfusions to stay alive and had been reduced from 190 pounds to about 90. Dr. Blais, his doctor, had earlier become a good friend because of my successful prosecution of a case involving his daughter as a victim.

Dr. Blais frankly told me that medically he was terminal and might, with transfusions, live in misery for no more than four or five weeks; without transfusions, less than two weeks. Either way he would be on morphine. I explained that Mother was still hoping for a miracle and that Pa, born in Crescent City, had confided to me that he wanted to die at home.

Pa was born in a home overlooking Lake Crescent and was living in a home on the shore of the same lake that had been a major part of his life. The home was south of the fishing resort and was on an adjacent twelve acres. The ride from home to fishing resort was about a quarter of a mile through the orange groves. I remembered that his grandson Jeff, Nelline's eldest, had wanted to chauffeur me from home to the resort in my shiny new Mercury Marquis when he was about eleven. The ride made Joey Chitwood, the famous daredevil driver, look like an amateur. At high rates of speed we would do a ninety degree turn to the right around an orange tree and then reverse with sand being kicked six feet high. The entire ride would see Jeff buckling over with laughter and I assumed for that reason he could not hear my frantic pleas to slow down. We arrived and Pa allowed only that my car needed a wash and rubbing compound to remove the scratches. Jeff could do no wrong in Pa's eyes.

Dr. Blais indicated that if we chose home he would teach me how to inject morphine in the proper amounts. Mama reluctantly agreed and we were driven home in an ambulance provided by the new Justice of the Peace (JP) who also owned the local funeral home and ambulance service. Harry, the driver, replaced his father as JP and he would later rely on my legal expertise. It was Harry who had called when Pa was shot. I had met the ambulance on the highway headed north to the hospital while I was headed south to pick up Mother. It had been a close call.

When we arrived in Crescent City I pulled back the curtain and a smile told me that I had done the right thing. Pa was much pleased that he would die at home.

Pa as a child had fired the boiler of a tug boat which ferried oranges from the east shore of Lake Crescent to Jacksonville. The boat was under the command of Capt. John Pigue, his father, and I believe that he was born in the same house that Pa was born in. Pa was in the Merchant Marines doing duty in the South Pacific during WW II. He had a ship shot out from under him but he survived and the Japanese Zero which sank the ship was shot down. He brought a tip of the Zero's prop home with him and later "lost" it in a card game to his nephew Wallace who had also served in the South Pacific as a Marine Captain. Wallace, the school principal in Daytona, recently (in the year 2000) gave me the prop tip knowing "that Les would have wanted you to have it".

Harry had provided a hospital bed and I moved in because Mother couldn't administer the morphine. The office staff could reach me by telephone. Mother, maybe for the first time in her life, was content for me to be in charge. I screened the visitors and visiting times. I called Dr. Blais because the prescribed morphine amounts were not keeping up with the pain. I was permitted to go on an as-needed basis. Mercy came and he died. I went to the grove to tell Mama that his pain was over. It was far and away the best attended funeral ever in Crescent City. Pa was fifty-eight when he died. Another "father" had left my life. The General was now my sole surviving "father".

Pa and the General had become good friends at Camp Blanding during the onset of WWII. The General had retired from the military and moved to Ormond Beach. He was a frequent visitor to Pigue's fishing resort during the late fifties and all of the sixties. That was where we became friends.

Sometime during 1972 General Thames called and asked me to stop by for high tea and meet his new next door neighbor. I did and high tea was dry red wine. The neighbor was Joseph M. France, Jr. and he with his family had recently moved from Maryland. Joe was an eye surgeon. We became instant friends and rapidly became pall bearer close. This Friday afternoon high tea was the original of "happy hour" at the General's.

It convened, with few exceptions, every Friday afternoon at 5 p.m. and lasted until 7:30 p.m. The core group rapidly expanded to over a dozen married couples and their children. Most were doctors, lawyers, judges or Indian chiefs. It was, of course, conceded by all that the Citra frog hunter was the apple of the General's eye. It was mostly social but we occasionally granted an audience to candidates for public office. It convened regularly for about twenty years.

During that twenty years and after, the core group was regularly expanded by children's marriages. This expanded "family" bonded to the point of being as close as blood kin. We shared and share good times and bad times. We alone could fill up a church, yard or banquet hall to attend a wedding, baptism, funeral or graduation party.

The General was from Jacksonville, a distinguished graduate of Clemson University and served as General MacArthur's Signal Corps Officer during the occupation of Japan. Following his military retirement he was employed by General Electric and, for them, was in charge of the Apollo support division charged with responsibility for quality control of all electronic communications. Miss Sara and I were given a piece of metal that went to the moon.

Only a few days before his death we visited with him while he was supposedly in a coma. We saw a smile and I knew he recognized my voice. He was much of a man and was my last "father."

21

Going gets tough; tough get going; a sheriff is removed

During the late fall, 1970, I began to receive reports from Dick Watson that prostitution houses and illegal numbers games then operated at will in areas around touristy St. Augustine.

I, as an Assistant State Attorney, had drafted a search warrant for a hunting lodge in St. Johns County where cock fights (illegal) were regularly held. The lodge was large and in its center was a round open fire place vented through an overhead hood. The fighting arena was placed on the fire place and the cock fight and betting began.

I had drawn the search warrant for some Attorney General investigators. The warrant was successful and I was told by the investigators that its execution resulted in an Assistant State Attorney from Jacksonville exiting, head first, through a closed window. He ran through the woods and was not caught but his car was left in the parking lot.

L.O. Davis, the sheriff of St Johns County, was the dean of all Florida sheriffs. He was then in his twenty-fifth year in office. I recalled that during one political rally in 1968 he had approached and offered his support on the condition that I "cross-deputize" the St. Johns County Constable as a State Attorney investigator. He didn't mention "if elected" and I suspected that the offer had been made to every State Attorney candidate in the race. His support was believed to garner many votes. I declined the offer.

Shortly after I began my term as State Attorney the St. Johns County Constable was arrested and convicted for solicitation of a bribe. Dick Watson prosecuted the case. The conviction was reversed on grounds that part of an incriminating taped telephone conversation was unintelligible. The case was returned to the trial court, the constable pled guilty to a lesser misdemeanor and was removed from office.

During my tenure as Assistant State Attorney I had a Flagler County case which required the testimony of Halstead "Hoss" Manucy. Manucy was the man who had defied the federal judge concerning injunctions issued during the 1964 Martin Luther King marches in St. Augustine. The subpoena was sent to the Sheriff's office of St. Johns County for service. It had been returned "unable to locate". The next day I had a conference with the Assistant State Attorney for St. Johns County concerning other matters. I arrived at his office and had to wait because he was having a conference with the sheriff and the unlocatable Halstead Manucy.

During late 1970 Dick Watson called and said that I should come to St. Augustine. The local bail bond runner had been caught red-handed doing the illegal *bolita* (numbers) game.

The runner "turned" and became a state witness. A taped telephone conversation between him and the sheriff was arranged and some very incriminating statements made by the sheriff were recorded. The defense during pretrial proceedings moved to suppress the tape. The motion was denied but during the later trial, after introduction of the tape in evidence, the trial judge did not allow the most incriminating portions to be heard by the jury. Watson and I had and have no explanation for that ruling.

The sheriff was indicted and suspended by the Governor. We prepared for the trial that took place during the Fall of 1970.

During the winter of 1969/1970 I with Miss Sara, Leslie and Stephen, Jr. attended the National District Attorneys Association three-day conference in Denver, Colorado. On the plane ride there some rough weather caused Stephen, Jr. to vomit in my lap, as had the boy on the rough ride over Atlanta returning from Lackland AFB.

The seminar included a half-day presentation on search and seizure by J. Shane Creamer. Only five minutes into his presentation I realized that he had to be among the top five most knowledgeable persons concerning Fourth Amendment issues and those issues were becoming ever more present in prosecutions. Prior police actions had created the exclusionary rule which simply excluded the jury from considering evidence that had been seized contrary to the Fourth Amendment.

We were to host the Florida Prosecuting Attorney Association (FPAA) fall educational conference in Daytona in the fall of 1972. During a break I asked if he could attend and be the centerpiece lecturer on search and seizure. I explained that attendees would be prosecutors and police. The next day he accepted and during our conversation I explained our pending prosecution of the sheriff of St. Johns County. He expressed an immediate interest and later was appointed by me as special assistant to the State Attorney and he attended the sheriff's trial in an advisory capacity.

On the eve of trial, surveillance indicated that a person on the jury *venire* had visited with the Sheriff but on inquiry of the prospective juror he denied any contact. We had to use a precious peremptory challenge. Our motion to change *venue* had been denied. During the early part of the trial one juror was overheard to say to another, "How much more of this shit do we have to listen to?" It seemed to underline that our motion to change *venue* had been well grounded.

The jury was out seven minutes and the Sheriff was acquitted. Selection of a foremen usually took longer than seven minutes. Most jurors shook his hand and patted him on the back. The foreman did both, asking if there was anything else he could do for his sheriff.

Immediately following the trial I packed all our evidence including that related to bawdy houses, *bolita* and cock fighting into multiple banker boxes. They were placed in my truck and I drove to Tallahassee that night wearing a concealed shoulder holster and weapon. I would seek an audience with the Governor's legal counsel to see if trial in the Senate on malfeasance and misfeasance had any possibility. I was new in the "political" arena and I knew that Claude Kirk the Republican Governor and the Sheriff shared many political supporters. I suspected that a decision to reinstate the Sheriff would be made tomorrow. I thought I had little chance.

The tenor of the times and the reason for the shoulder holster can best be explained by a case I prosecuted in St. Augustine near in time to the prosecution of the sheriff. Floyd Boatwright had been the local bail bondsman and Warnock Tedder had been his "runner." Floyd Boatwright didn't need bounty hunters. He was strong, large and brutal and, at least in those days, bail bondsmen had power to seize and return absconding defendants and bail jumpers from any state in the Union.

Pursuant to such powers and his abilities he had retrieved three young locals from Texas and had deposited their souls in the St. Johns County jail. I recalled that he had personally, and alone, manhandled them back to Florida. Having served their time, they were on the street.

The case I tried involved allegations that, soon after their release, they were knocking on the front door of the Floyd Boatwright residence, and after he appeared each shot him several times in cold blood. He was instantly dead.

In the sheriff's case I called the Governor's office in less than a minute after it opened. I asked for Mr. Mager, the governor's legal counsel, and he came on line. I requested an audience and informed him of its purpose.

I drove to the old Capitol building and loaded my boxes onto a dolly. I entered his office with the dolly and was permitted to sit down. I started to make my case and he raised a hand and said, "The Governor will keep him suspended and refer the matter to the Senate on one condition" and that was that I, not he, would present the case. I accepted. We shook hands and I left not having opened a single banker's box. That St. Johns County was, law-enforcement-wise, out of control was better known than I thought.

The procedure in the Senate required that the evidence must first be presented and heard by the Select Committee on Suspensions. The proceedings were less formal than the courtroom and did not require strict adherence to the evidence code. The chairman of the committee ruled on objections. He happened to be Fred Karl who was elected Volusia Senator when I was elected State Attorney. He was a well-respected lawyer and we had shared many political podiums.

The thrust of my case was that prostitution, illegal gambling and illegal cockfighting could not thrive unless the Sheriff was at least looking the other way. Proving malfeasance and misfeasance did not require proof of bribes. My case took about a week and the Sheriff's defense was that he had no knowledge of such things and would surely attend to them when he returned. The hearing ended and a Senator on the committee called me aside. He explained that during a recess the Sheriff had called him aside to explain that his trip to a bawdy house in St. Johns County was made only to see if suspicion that a deputy was homosexual was true.

The committee voted unanimously to recommend to the full Senate that the Governor's suspension should be sustained.

I was in the gallery when the Senate received and debated the committee report. Senator Verle Pope from St. Augustine, "the lion of the Senate", rose to speak. He was past President of the Senate and then chaired the Appropriations Committee. He was by far the best orator there. He had at one time publicly referred to the governor as "Claude Quirk." He now allowed that some Senators had suggested that he allow them to speak for him because the young State Attorney who had presented the matter before the committee was his first cousin once removed and that they both had spent considerable time in Island Grove, *albeit* at far different times. He further indicated that because his parents were born deaf, he had learned to talk at his grandparents' knees in Island Grove. The grandmother of the Senator was the great-grandmother of the young cousin State Attorney. She was a Carlton and that clan had produced a former Governor, Doyle E. Carlton. He further warmed up by "confessing" that he knew there were Senators here who believed that Senate business would be expedited if he still spoke in sign language. He responded to his confession by noting that the melody of his oratory fell softly and sweetly upon his own ears. I noted that I could be no better than third best in family speech-making.

Closely in time to this proceeding Dick Watson and I had

argued an appeal to a bond validation in the Supreme Court of Florida. Our wives had accompanied us to marvel at the talents of these two legal warriors. Following these arguments we had coffee in chambers with the justices and they included Justice Vasser Carlton. Cousin Vasser had recently been elevated from Circuit Judge in the 18th Judicial Circuit. I introduced Sally to the cousin and she was taken aback that he sported a large chaw of tobacco which frequently required a trip to his nearby spittoon. He also was a cousin to cousin Verle.

Senator Pope then politely rejected the idea that others speak for him and noted that, since learning to speak, he had never suffered from lack of words and only *his* words could truly speak *his* mind. He went on and I suddenly realized that his defense of the relationship (ours) was, in reality, a credibility builder for his young cousin prosecutor. He was followed by the Senator who told of the Sheriff's bawdy house trip.

The vote was forty-eight to two in favor of sustaining the Governor's suspension. The vote removed the Sheriff from office. The body politic only needed a catalyst and he had come from Citra. I paid a courtesy visit to Mr. Mager who had become "Gerry". We were friends and he wanted to know if I would accept specially assigned cases in other circuits. I agreed and would begin multiple special assignments to be served for this Governor and the next two. They would include investigations of judges, a State Attorney, Sheriffs, County Commissioners and School Board members.

The Governor, Claude Kirk, wanted to meet the lion killer; Gerry inquired, "Do you have time?" I didn't know the Governor rose to about six feet four inches. He already had a tummy and he had little military bearing. But this man, for reasons still unknown to me, had put in motion a process that would badly bend, if not break, the worst "good ole boy" system in north Florida. He also appointed Gerry to an appellate court before leaving office and I would be invited and attend his investiture.

I drove home musing that my present circumstances, shoulder holster included, must mean that I was at least a distant cousin to Elliott Ness but I didn't know if Ness was Anglo-Saxon. I arrived home and apologized to Miss Sara for my lateness noting that the delay was caused by the Governor's wanting to meet me. I got the look but no kick.

During that trip home I also mused over the fact that the author of *Cross Creek* was a "best" friend to Peggy Watson's mother and that she also had been a writer. Ms. Rawlins was, in fact, Peggy's Godmother and was married to Norton Baskin. We had met Norton Baskin (I never saw him in Island Grove) at a small dinner party at cousin Verle's home. He was in a silk suit with a Panama hat. His hands were uncalloused, unscarred and his nails were professionally manicured. I noticed that the face and neck revealed no signs of a skin blemished by the outdoor Florida sun. His conversations were genteel and almost wholly with the ladies. Miss Sara thought he was the most charming, well-mannered and interesting man, including me, whom she had ever met. Mr. Baskin gave every appearance of being a "Dandy" but I later learned from reading the biography of Ms. Rawlings that, way over draft age, he had volunteered to (and did) drive an ambulance in the Far East war zone during World War II.

During the fall (1972) FPAA conference in Daytona Shane Creamer was awesome. We had become friends immediately and shared many views on the proper roles and relationships of the agencies involved in criminal justice.

During my stay at Moody AFB I had become aware of the book *Ruby McCollum* which could not be bought in Florida. It was a book written by an author concerning a black female *bolita* operator in Live Oak, Florida who had an ongoing love affair with a local Caucasian doctor. The doctor was killed and she was tried for the murder.

I mention this because following Shane's presentation Miss Sara and I had dinner with about eight State Attorneys and Shane. One of the State Attorneys was Randall Slaughter, State Attorney of the Third Circuit which included Suwanee County which, in turn, included Live Oak as its county seat. Randall always wore red socks, was a senior orator from the old school and was always entertaining. I did not know the source but he and Governor Kirk had serious disagreements which finally resulted in Randall's resignation. At the news conference concerning the resignation all the questions amounted to, "Why are you resigning, Mr. Slaughter?" and his only answer was, "I don't have to take this shit any more."

We had a treat in store. Randall had become the State Attorney of the Third Circuit after the Ruby McCollum affair shocked Live Oak. Randall entertained us about three hours with all the details.

My letter to Shane Creamer adds to what happened in the Senate hearing. It read as follows:

I received your letter of November 10, 1970. The turmoil and shouting has not completely subsided. We represented the Governor in a suspension hearing in Tallahassee this week. After the trial we were successful in having the Governor amend the suspension order on the grounds of misfeasance, malfeasance, etc. We were then appointed to present the case to the Senate Suspension Committee. On Monday, November 16, 1970, the Senate committee will make their recommendation to the full Senate. The full

Senate will then decide the question. We do not know the Senate committee's recommendation. We do know that it was quite an experience presenting the matter to the Senate committee. We do know that we are tired.

I have no regrets and I know that Dick Watson has no regrets.

During the course of the Senate committee hearing Mr. Davis and his counsel presented a signed statement from the trial jury. The statement indicated that the trial jury thought the Senate committee or the State was conducting a vendetta. The statement also indicated that the Senate hearing was an attack on the integrity of the *petit* jury. When this statement was offered by Mr. Davis and his attorneys it clearly had an effect they did not anticipate. The chairman of the committee immediately inquired concerning the circumstances of the preparation of the statement. Mr. Frank Howath, representing Davis at the hearing, indicated that he had prepared the statement from information furnished by the Sheriff. Mr. Harold Wayne, Tax Assessor for St. Johns County and close friend of L.O. Davis, (not admitted to the Florida Bar but assisting in Davis' representation by the grace of the committee) indicated that he had had no hand in the preparation of the statement. The chairman immediately issued subpoenaes for two of the jurors that had signed the statement. They appeared and the foreman of the jury testified that the statement was presented to him by the Sheriff, and that he signed it as presented. He indicated that he had never been consulted concerning the language in the statement. The other juror likewise indicated that he had never been consulted about the language in the statement. During the course of the trial jury foreman's testimony he indicated that he had talked to the sheriff shortly after the acquittal and had indicated to him that he hoped this would be the end of the matter, but if there were other repercussions he would be glad to assist in any way possible. He also testified to his long-standing friendship with the Sheriff. As a result of this testimony there should be no doubt in the committee's mind about the hopelessness of the State's case at the trial level. The seven minute verdict together with this testimony seems to indicate that we had substantially less than a fair and impartial jury. Despite all this I still have no better system to offer. I think that the over-all operation of the jury system is the fairest known to mankind to date.

There can be no question about the friendship from this end. Dick and I will be forever grateful for your assistance. We will, likewise, always be in touch and available for any assistance we may render you. I will be talking with Dick in the near future and we will set the training seminar shortly. You can depend on being the star of the show. I will appreciate any indication you may have of a date agreeable with you.

I will drop you a note around Tuesday on the Senate's action. My best to you and your family.

During December, 1970 Shane was appointed Attorney General for the Commonwealth of Pennsylvania.

22

The go-to prosecutor for three governors; investigates state treasurer

1972 went almost uneventfully. I practiced law and prosecuted "common" murders, rapes and robberies. The softball games and piano recitals increased, and the wannabee architect's plans had produced a very comfortable and attractive home in the neighborhood of 4500 square feet without including porches. Miss Sara had been "freed" from trailer living. SLB Jr., his friend Bobby and I often attended NASCAR auto and motorcycle races in Daytona. The trips included loading of their mini-bikes on the pick-up and allowing them to ride on the rural dirt roads near Haw Creek in rural Flagler County.

Two events did occur at about the same time. The general election included the passage of Article V and that article drastically changed the court system. Circuit Courts were given jurisdiction over probate, juvenile and dependency proceedings. State Attorneys would uniformly prosecute juveniles in Circuit Court and misdemeanors in County Court. This would be a substantial increase in caseload requiring about twice the staff as under the old system. Administration and budgeting would consume much more of the State Attorney's time.

The second event was that the State Attorney would have to become full time in January of 1973. I had been unopposed for my second term but I had to decide whether to leave

Miss Kate and be State Attorney or exclusively practice with her. It was an agonizing decision. The State Attorney pay would almost double and it included some substantial benefits. Miss Kate had the resources to practice law any way she liked, but if she retired, I would not have that luxury because of the needs of a large family. Miss Kate had already instructed me to let her know when her "time" came to retire. She did not want to go "past" that time. I would then essentially be doing probate and real estate because I had little interest in civil litigation and a lot of our real estate work was *pro bono* (free) for our extended families. I selected being a full time State Attorney.

Despite Miss Kate's and my parting as law partners, the relationship between our families continued to grow closer and closer. Several years later we paid our final tribute to this great lady. One of her nephews was William L. Townsend, Jr. Returning from combat in Vietnam, he also had become her law partner. I was told by Bill that she went parasailing not too long before her death and, not surprisingly, she soared like an eagle. Following her death, Sally and I would join her nieces and nephews and the extended family to complete the burning of an upright live oak trunk killed by lighting. It was near her front door and when the mood struck she would set it afire, burn a little and then douse. It made a huge fire while we sipped and shared memories of this grand lady. The good Lord threw away the mold when she was created. The tree became red coals and embers and the riderless horse was out of view.

During the 1972 holiday period Miss Sara and I were somewhere in the circuit at a close friend's home for a Christmas party. Another good friend guest pulled me aside and allowed that when I got her to vote and support Reuben Askew for Governor I had told her that he was an honest man. (Governor Askew was, at that time, Reuben who? and I was one of a very few elected public officials climbing on his "wagon.") I reaffirmed that he was and asked, "What are you talking about?"

She explained that she and her husband, a member of the Florida Petroleum Marketers Association (FPMA), had recently attended their annual meeting in Orlando. During the conference they were told that the only way to keep Florida free of self-serve gasoline was to make a contribution to the recently-elected State Treasurer, Thomas O'Malley, who as State Fire Marshall could keep in place a regulation that self-serve gas was a fire hazard. They were told the hat would be passed, it was, and almost $41,000 in required cash was collected and transferred to Tallahassee. The lady knew that it was wrong. I explained that cabinet officers in Florida were elected state-wide, and were not really superintended by the Governor in their prescribed duties.

The husband, also a close friend, arrived and wanted to know what his wife had been telling his friend the State Attorney. I explained what I had learned, she got a "did-you-have-to-do-that?" look and I explained that Treasurer O'Malley had recently been elected, had not announced as a candidate four years hence and beyond reasonable doubt had not opened a campaign account. I explained that campaign donations had to be by check, including the name and address of the contributor, and for amounts over $100 had to include the contributor's occupation. He knew that because he had contributed to my campaigns.

I requested that he gather the names and addresses of the twelve or fifteen members who would be able to provide material evidence and meet me in his office, after business hours, the next day. He consented, and I avoided the unpleasant task of putting him under subpoena for a State Attorney investigation. The meeting went as planned and I advised that he could be my confidential informant (CI), which worked well because I would need other information. He had done his homework and I got the witnesses and their addresses.

About ten days later the witnesses, pursuant to subpoena, arrived at the City Island Courthouse Annex in Daytona Beach. They were all wanting to know, "What's this all about?". I, with a court reporter, took their testimony one by one and the truth came out. Some said they thought it was a campaign contribution and I asked why, citing the matters explained to the CI. I got transcripts of the testimony and called the Governor's Legal Counsel Edgar M. Dunn, Jr. and requested a meeting. Ed had worked for me as an Assistant State Attorney and at my behest had been active in the Askew campaign. He was from an old and respected Daytona family and they had enormous success in business primarily due to their hard work and thrift. Dunns Creek had been named for his first-arriving kin.

I met with Ed and let him read the transcripts of testimony. I explained that I had some concerns about *venue* since the obvious *venue* was only Orlando or Tallahassee. I explained that further investigation might reveal the money had been taken (delay *en route*) to Volusia. He gave me a "wow" and said he would call after talking to the Governor and that, by the way, I had been selected as a Florida member to attend the National Conference on Criminal Justice to be held in Washington, D.C. during March, 1973. I got the call indicating that he, the Governor and I would discuss the matter in Washington. The seventies' version of a small-town Elliott Ness was again on the prowl.

During the meeting with the Governor in Washington I learned that they believed proper *venue* would be in Leon County which included Tallahassee, and that another State Attorney would be specially assigned to complete the investigation. The Governor had earlier indicated that I was being specially assigned to an investigation in Dade County which would occupy about half my time. Governors were now vying for my time and that did nothing to dampen the enthusiasm of the State Attorney from Citra.

Miss Sara and I had taken the train to Washington and had brought Leslie, Stephen and Allyson. There was no shortage of grandparents to take care of Corinne Adele who had been born in March, 1971."Dell" was aptly named. She had the best traits of both grandmothers, and in particular she was as straight forward, honest and moral as my mother. She would later obtain a degree in resource conservation from the University of Florida, and a masters degree from The University of North Florida. She would be employed by the Department of Environmental Protection. Her job would keep her in the woods and on the lakes roamed by her father as a boy. She would marry Dennis Mills, a timber producer, and they would produce Cody Lane and Savannah Grace.

During our time in Washington most of my hours were taken up by attendance and study. Miss Sara and the kids watched the funeral procession of President Johnson and together we all toured *the* Supreme Court building after being searched at the main entrance. The conference over, we toured the Washington Zoo and saw the pandas. We exited the back gate at closing time because I knew it was about a mile closer to the hotel. We entered what had to be one of the highest-crime-rate districts in the nation. The gate was closed and there was no turning back. I dealt with scofflaws and multi-convicted felons on a daily basis and I suspected that we passed over two hundred waiting for their next prey. We "strolled" and I watched their eye movements. I suddenly realized that they thought this was surely a police "set-up" and we were not bothered.

On the ride home I began to read some of the materials concerning the Dade County assignment. I didn't mind the assignment but I did mind having to spend substantial time in Miami. The last time I had been there was in the spring of 1960 to take the three-day bar exam. I simply didn't like to be in fast-paced large cities with traffic congestion and nearly everything crowded. I didn't like balmy weather and the assignment would include dodging thunderstorms in the (Florida) Cabinet jet. Miss Sara and the two oldest children would stay with the prosecutors in the Doral Country Club, provided by Dade County, and they would be tutored in tennis by Arthur Ashe.

The investigation resulted in the prosecution of one judge. He was defended by one with trial lawyer talents equal to my mentor, Major Murphy. He later became Chief Justice of the Florida Supreme Court. His name was Gerald Kogan. Jimmy Russell, State Attorney (SA) of the Sixth Judicial Circuit (Pinellas and Pasco Counties) had been assigned to assist me in this special assignment. "Jimma", upon the completion of my closing argument, had whispered, "That's one of, if not the best, closing arguments I have ever heard and I don't think I could have done it". Richard Mench and Bernie McCabe, two of Jimma's assistants, were also present for this revelation and we, knowing Jimma as we did, unanimously concluded that this was the first and last time that Jimma would admit that someone had exceeded his talents in the courtroom. Justice Kogan and I left the courtroom with great mutual respect and became good friends. His client was acquitted.

My career and my parenting were suffering some incompatibility and these family trips provided some reconciliation. Dell on one occasion ran to the TV when told by her mother "There's daddy." Daddy was at the back door. On another occasion I left home on a Sunday afternoon to board a plane to somewhere to do a special assignment. Miss Sara was digging in the sewer line to unplug a clog. "Honey, I'll be at the Hilton if you need me."

During one trip home from Miami I contacted the assigned State Attorney and learned that there would be no prosecution resulting from the FPMA investigation. He explained that the money was given to Treasurer O'Malley's legal counsel, State employed, and that he, not knowing what the money was for, had placed it under his bed. He later returned most of the money to the FPMA. I didn't get any details on whether they had identified the bag man and whether they had put him under oath to testify about where the delivery was made and what he and the legal counsel had said. There was no mention concerning the form of the return of the money but I suspected it was a personal check on the account of the legal counsel. I was wondering if they ever considered granting immunity to legal counsel for his truthful testimony. I was wondering if they ever took the testimony of the hat-passer in Orlando.

I suspected that this investigation had been turned over to a non-lawyer investigator who had neither the skills nor determination to unearth such matters. Added to that was the intimidation that such a person would feel in the presence of such "high and mighty" figures. My minor immodesty permitted me the conclusion that I would have made the case perhaps only because I had not sense enough to fear such things. My Corinne-Lloyd legacy was earning me many enemies.

Sometime during the mid-seventies an annual physical revealed a heart irregularity which the family physician could not diagnose. He sent me to North Florida Regional in Gainesville for a cardiac catheterization. The cardiologist indicated that it was only a minor weakening of the lower right ventricle and it was not uncommon in men my "age." He said it required no treatment, no medication and that I should avoid stress!

23

'Bloody Sunset in St. Augustine'; Prosecution of Alan Stanford

During the evening of January 23, 1974 Dick Watson called me to St. Augustine because a woman had had her head almost severed with a machete. The suspect was her neighbor, the County Manager. His name was Alan Stanford. The crime had taken place on her front steps and it was a truly gruesome scene. It was so gruesome that the initial ambulance attendant had washed down the blood with a garden hose.

Dick and I agreed that he would monitor/assist in the investigation and keep me informed. The investigation ultimately produced written statements of witnesses and sworn testimony. It also produced tangible items of evidence. The investigation was attended and impeded by massive publicity. Later the incident and the trial of Alan Stanford became a very successful book entitled *Bloody Sunset in St. Augustine*. The co-authors were Jim Mast and Nancy Powell. The case was also featured on the television show "City Confidential." I will therefore limit my account of the matter to a condensed version as seen by the prosecutor.

Athalia Ponsell Lindsley was the victim and she was a relative newcomer to St. Augustine. She had been a fashion model in New York and had, among others, been courted by Tyrone Power and Joseph Kennedy, Jr. She was then married to a former mayor of St. Augustine and had a home on Marine Street. She was then in her fifties and she and the ex-Mayor had separate residences. Her residence overlooked the Intracoastal Waterway, "a bay," and faced easterly.

Her close neighbor to the north was a home occupied by the McCormicks, consisting of mother, father, and son Locke. Mrs. McCormick's mother lived across the street. The son was then in his mid to late teens.

Ms. Lindsley's southerly neighbors were Alan Stanford, his wife and several daughters. Alan Stanford was the County Manager and a marine engineer but not yet certified as a civil engineer so that he could become County Engineer with higher pay than County Manager.

Ms. Lindsley's adjacent neighbors had both complained about her barking dogs and even sued her over the matter. I note that barking dogs, for close neighbors, have been the motive for many confrontations and crimes in American jurisprudence. It ranks up there with the emotions involved in boundary line disputes which many times involve only inches of soil.

The Stanford/Lindsley relationship involved much more. Ms. Lindsley, a sort of pro-active gadfly, was on Stanford's case concerning his credentials and abilities as County Manager. She was his frequent critic at County Commission meetings and her complaints were that he was incompetent to supervise road construction and that he was signing papers as "County Engineer" when he was only authorized to sign as "County Manager." The meetings were vitriolic and included her accusation that he had threatened to kill her. Her real thrust was to ask that he be dismissed as unqualified and incompetent. The last such meeting occurred one day before her death. On January 23, 1974, investigators for the Florida Board of

Professional Engineers had visited Stanford and explained that there were complaints he was violating law by signing as "County Engineer." I don't think that anyone in St. Johns County, including Stanford, ever doubted the authorship of those complaints. Stanford's itinerary on the afternoon of the murder would be a serious issue at the trial.

At almost precisely 6 p.m. on January 23, 1974 Mrs. Lindsley was hacked to death on her front porch by an assailant wielding a machete. Locke McCormick had heard the noise--"chopping"--and had gone to the front yard of the Lindsley residence and observed the murder. He excitedly exclaimed to his mother that "Mr. Stanford is hitting Ms. Ponsell"; the recent marriage to Lindsley was apparently unknown to him. Stanford's wife would later testify at trial that she had heard a "noise" and had run out her back door. Locke's testimony was that the assailant had taken a south-westerly exit which could only lead to Stanford's garage at the rear of his house. Stanford's wife's testimony admitted, in my mind, that she had seen the assailant because the geographics and timing would not permit otherwise. She was, within minutes, exiting her front door to talk with Locke's mother.

I thought that this evidence alone was sufficient to identify the assailant. The trial defense which included the 'Dewey Lee' conspiracy would only be a red herring. Dewey Lee was the one who found the clothes, watch and machete in the nearby marsh and the defendant's version would have included a near-impossible and inconceivable conspiracy between him and the investigating officers to share the princely sum of $500 (the reward money). But as in the L.O. Davis case we were not playing on level ground. Verdicts had to be unanimous and we were dealing with a *venire* that was already about 50/50 on guilt or innocence because of massive publicity and small-town gossip. In the Introduction to *Bloody Sunset* the trial judge, Gene Eastmoore, put it this way: ". . .There were those who believed he was innocent, those who believed he was guilty and those who believed she (the victim) deserved what she got."

Stanford had become a Vestryman at Trinity Episcopal Church and he was a popular figure in the county. He was not so popular with his subordinate county employees. Ms. Lindsley on the other hand was essentially a "carpet-bagger" with very liberal views which she espoused often in a very conservative atmosphere.

The parish priest at Trinity, spearheaded the raising of the Stanford defense fund and it split the church. The publicity and rumor had split the town and the county. Why had the trial judge not granted our motion for change of *venue* considering the burden that the unanimity law placed on the prosecution? Only one reasonable doubt could "hang" the jury. He chose the safe way of not ruling on the change until *voir dire* (questioning prospective jurors concerning their knowledge of the case and their ability to be impartial). Prospective jurors often find it embarrassing to admit partiality.

As I have indicated, Dewey Lee, a Road Department employee, had found a machete, a watch repaired for Stanford earlier, a pair of shoes and bloody clothes matching those Stanford had worn on the day of the murder. The items were found in a marsh near Stanford's home and their actual location was not far from a boathouse used by Stanford. The evidence at trial would show that he had borrowed a machete from the County barn which was never returned.

We went to trial and put on our case hoping the actual evidence would overcome rumor and publicity. The exclamation by Locke was not publicly known and had not made the press. We thought that it would be powerfully persuasive because the law recognizes statements under exciting circumstances can be used as evidence to prove the truth of the excited utterance. Such statements often carry more weight than in-court testimony. Locke and his father had been fishing with Stanford while he was on bail and we thought that would explain his reluctance to make a clear in-court identification. He still lived only one house away from Stanford.

We introduced the items found in the marsh and believed they were powerfully persuasive. We knew the defense would have to resort to a conspiracy theory to disconnect Stanford from those items and we knew that such a defense had no factual basis. The defense lawyers would have to raise it by cross examination, innuendo and argument. We thought it was frivolous because it rested on the assumption that police officers searching Stanford's home the day after the murder had taken these items and soaked them in blood. They or Dewey Lee would have then placed them in the marsh hoping that they would later produce reward money. We thought the jury would see it as frivolous and on the evidence presented they would have no doubt. The defense unfolded as we expected.

The only other defense would be alibi, which would include Stanford's testimony. We thought it would fail because it depended on the memory of witnesses concerning exact times they had seen Stanford's county car at the county barn or exact times they had seen him driving the car. *Bloody Sunset* has accurately reported these issues at the trial:

> Stephen Boyles, the blue-eyed prosecutor who opened the state's arguments, hammered away at the "flaws" in Stanford's alibi and waved the numerous contradictions in the testimony of defense witnesses like red flags at the jury. Boyles implied that some of the witnesses, including

Mrs. Stanford, had not told the truth. However, none of the trial witnesses ever were charged with perjury.

Boyles stood before the jury, dressed in a blue and white striped seersucker suit that matched his large, piercing eyes, to begin painting a graphic picture of what he believed actually happened that terrible night Athalia Lindsley lost her life. He pictured Stanford as driving home from the office in a great state of anger following the visit by two men from the state who were investigating a complaint signed by Mrs. Lindsley. Boyles emphasized that the two men testified they had told Stanford he must stop signing county documents as a civil engineer. "Things were closing in," Boyles declared. "Mrs. Lindsley was about to get his job."

Boyles paused, giving jurors time to think about it. Then, he began to review Stanford's testimony. Stanford had come home from the office and poured himself a gin and tonic, understandable after a stressful day. Stanford had admitted to mixing a second drink and in Boyles' version of the story, he "probably had consumed a third drink before looking out the window and spotting Athalia in the yard. With two or three drinks to fortify him, Stanford had gone to the garage, grabbed the machete he had borrowed from the county, and walked over there to her, literally hacking the poor woman to death."

Boyles paused for a second time, watching jurors' expressions for reaction, but their faces were like stone.

"Athalia Ponsell Lindsey had a right to live no matter how much she had antagonized Stanford," Boyles said. "But, NOBODY deserves what SHE GOT," Boyles shouted and pounded the lectern, then paused again before continuing his version of the death scene.

At six o'clock on January 23, 1974, Alan Stanford was so enraged by Athalia's meddling in his life, "he did not care whether he was seen or not when he walked across the yead and began swinging the machete. In his state of mind, he didn't care who saw him," Boyles told the jury, in a strident voice, a decibel softer than a yell. The prosecutor speculated that Stanford had finished off Athalia and was walking around the side of the house when his wife ran out the back door. Mrs. Stanford had testified she ran out when she heard screaming but had not seen anyone, he said.

"If she ran out the back, she had to see the killer coming around the house carrying a machete, dripping with blood. Whom did she see? I tell you she saw her husband- -the defendant." Boyles turned away from the jury box and pointed a finger at Stanford.

Boyles theorized that Stanford had heard Rosemary McCormick calling his name and had told his wife to go back inside and out the front door to keep Mrs. McCormick occupied "out front" while he went into the garage to wash up and change clothes. There had been testimony there was a sink in an area of the garage Stanford used as a workshop and that laundry was kept in the garage. It had been easy enough for Stanford to remove his blood-splattered clothes without going into the house; stash them in a plastic bag; wipe and wrap the machete, and, after re-dressing, using clothes in the laundry bag before fleeing in the county car to the marsh a few blocks away, Boyles theorized. It was logical, Boyles continued, that Stanford would think of the marsh as a good spot to dump the evidence because he had testified that he kept his boat at a nearby boatyard.

"He knew where to go," Boyles said, gesturing like a maestro, before concluding that Stanford's decision to murder Athalia Lindsley was premeditated or "he wouldn't have hit her so many times or as viciously as he did."

Jurors sat poker-faced as Boyles cautioned them to "use your collective common sense, judgement and reasoning in deciding what evidence to accept and what to discard."

He said it was only natural for the jurors to have sympathy for the former county manager's family but he warned them not to stretch that sympathy "and strain your mind into eclipses of speculative doubt."

Boyles described Athalia as "a strong-willed woman" who spoke her piece but was doing nothing more than exercising her right to free speech when she attacked Stanford's professional credentials at county commission meetings. Locke McCormick, the young man who had seen the attack on Athalia, was as fair as he could be to both the state and the defendant when he testified "he could not swear Stanford was the murderer," Boyles said.

Standford was found not guilty.

Also from *Bloody Sunset:*

At least one of the jurors who set Stanford free needed reassurance that the panel had handed down the right verdict. The morning after the trial ended, a juror, Charles Rowley, who worked as an exterminator for Florida Pest Control, went directly to the home of Judge Eugene Eastmoore in Palatka. The Eastmoore home was one of the houses Rowley serviced.

The judge was still sleeping when Rowley came to the door and spoke with Eastmoore's wife. Rowley told her the jury had been troubled over the difference in the sizes of the shoes found in the marsh and the shoes Stanford wore at the trial. The discarded pair was a size 9½ D. The shoes Stanford wore were size 10 C but the actual difference was only an eighth of an inch.

Six months later, Eastmoore received a call from an insurance company, checking on a claim on a watch Stanford had filed. The company wanted to verify that the watch had been seized as evidence in a murder trial.

One could wonder why "trouble" over a 1/8 inch difference in shoe size was not erased by the laundry-marked shirt and the jeweler-marked watch. I believed then and I believe now that the evidence was inconsistent with any fact other than the defendant's guilt.

24

Profile of a prosecutor's office; Mama's death

I ran unopposed in 1976 and had given some thought to running for Attorney General and then maybe Governor. I already had some statewide connections including the other 19 State Attorneys and the Governor, and I had many, many cousins around the state. Once again we did it Miss Sara's way. We lived in a wonderful country home, the kids were in school and other activities, they had close friends and they were only minutes away from the grandparents. I remembered my and Nelline's snit at being moved only forty miles. Leslie was nearing high school graduation and Stephen was right behind. The wise woman who had been carted off to Newfoundland kept a tight rein and saved me from my mistakes.

This four-year term was mostly about special assignments statewide and managing a growing office. We now had about thirty Assistant State Attorneys and support personnel numbering about thirty-five. I had seven Division Chiefs and six of those supervised respective offices with geographically-designated divisions in Daytona, Deland, New Smyrna, Palatka, Bunnell and St. Augustine. The seventh was "Special Prosecutions", which was always located in whatever building I was in. Courthouse space problems moved my office five or six times during my stay. "Special Prosecutions" handled circuit-wide investigations, prosecutions of public officials, white collar fraud including land fraud and organized crime.

I could no longer handle all the charging decisions and they were delegated to the Division Chiefs. I usually did attend, as legal advisor, the grand jury proceedings in all four counties. The grand juries made the charging decision in capital cases which were now restricted to murder in the first degree. Their decision to charge, by law, was only based on probable cause and defense lawyers often wailed that a grand jury would indict an unnamed hot dog if so advised by the State Attorney. I had never advised or even suggested that a grand jury indict or not indict. When they had heard the evidence I advised them on the elements of the offense and any lesser included offences and explained probable cause. Whether the evidence met that standard was their decision, and I left the room. Their deliberations and vote were completely secret.

Probable cause was usually defined as "facts or apparent facts, including hearsay, which would lead a reasonable person to conclude that a person had probably committed the crime". The charging decision for the grand jury was an indictment if there was enough probable cause or a 'no true bill' when probable cause was lacking.

Explicitly or implicitly it is required by the U.S. Constitution that no person be found guilty unless the evidence convinces the fact finder, usually a trial jury, of guilt beyond any reasonable doubt. The discussions preceding the adoption of the Bill of Rights had produced an almost unanimous conclusion that it was better that some guilty go free in order that no innocent be convicted. This was the end of Star Chamber-like proceedings for the colonist under the rule of an arbitrary king. The only real discussion seemed to be "how many guilty go free before an innocent be convicted."

It was thus clear to me that a prosecution should not be launched with only probable cause. Probable cause was sufficient for the grand jury, for an arrest warrant and for a felony arrest without warrant. The charging instrument for the State Attorney was an "information" and the instrument denoting no prosecution was a "no information." I had early-on adopted the UCMJ form for the charge and specification of the charge and it is still used today.

I adopted, by a guidelines manual, a higher burden of proof for my Division Chiefs to initiate prosecutions. It was that before signing the information they had to have credible and admissible evidence, in hand, to get the case beyond a directed verdict, that is, that it was a legally sufficient case to go to the jury. I believed then, and still do, that it is the only policy that squares with the Bill of Rights. I add that it was not then, nor now, a universal prosecutorial approach but for our office it drew the line for law enforcement to get their product into court. We would often, however, assist in further investigation to get the case up to par. It was a policy readily accepted by the judges because they did not have to assume the unpopular burden of dismissing a bad case. It was an unpopular policy for the lazy or over-zealous law enforcement officer.

Our policy was known to all new Assistant State Attorneys before they were sworn in. Our hiring policies included a Division Chief nomination of three persons to fill a vacancy or new position. The three were then interviewed by the State Attorney and one or more Division Chiefs. The first question was, "Is the exclusionary rule constitutionally required, and if not, when and how did it come about?" The Division Chiefs present always smiled as they observed the tightening of a puckering string. Experience had taught that few had a clue but we were more interested in how they "thought on their feet."

The second question began with a reading of the printed certification of the information that "...this prosecution is brought in good faith..." and what did that mean? About seventy percent of the time the puckering string here snapped. The correct answer was, of course, our charging policy which was always read, from the manual, to each wannabe Assistant State Attorney.

1980 produced an opponent in the primary but I won, circuit-wide, by more than a three to one margin. The office continued to grow and I became more consumed with administrative matters. Most of my courtroom time was on special assignments by the Governor.

1980 did include a prosecution against Sidney L. Jaffe for land fraud and his retrieval (by bounty hunters) from Canada was "made" into an "international incident" by some powerful but ill-informed politicians. They included the Secretary of State and the Attorney General of the United States (and their counterparts in Canada). Their efforts to free Jaffe "encountered" the ire of a piney-woods prosecutor. This tale is told in the next chapter.

During the early spring of 1982 Miss Sara and I were in Hiawassee for a long weekend with Nelline and Roy. Mother called and stated that she was not feeling well and that I should come home. She did not elaborate but the tone was serious. We went home and I went to her home. I could see that she was very sick and on the same day the family doctor indicated that he strongly suspected cancer.

I called Nelline and made arrangements for her admission to Ormond Beach Memorial Hospital in Ormond. She was admitted and the existence of cancer was confirmed. Nelline arrived and we secured permission to sleep in the oncology visitors room. Nelline explained that she had a mechanical problem with her car and needed to tend to that. Mama said that it was a man's job and that Nelline should stay with her while Lewis tended to the car. I, from the tone and manner of her statement, eerily felt that she was reliving the Island Grove days after Daddy's death and we were to play (or were playing) the male and female roles. She was under heavy medication.

Nelline and I attended her in shifts. I took the night shift so that I could go to the office during the day. Mama died on April 22, 1982. The General had offered to house her in his home if she could leave the hospital. She and my father have never been far from my mind.

25

The Sidney Jaffe saga;
piney woods prosecutor strains
American/Canadian relations

Early in 1972 Continental Southeast Land Corporation
(CSELC) was formed and acquired ranch land in Southern
Putnam County consisting of more than 2000 acres. It
subdivided the land and began to sell lots to people who
resided all over the United States and Canada. The sales were
done with an unrecorded agreement for deed that promised a
warranty deed when all the purchase price had been paid.
The agreements for deed were paid on a monthly installment
basis. The corporation had also induced others to invest and
receive mortgage notes and it was also indebted by what
amounted to its original purchase money mortgage. It also
had unpaid taxes and other liens.

By 1976 Continental was substantially insolvent in that
its liabilities exceeded its assets by approximately two and
one half million dollars. Sydney L. Jaffe, who then owned
and/or controlled a half dozen or so corporations, had one of
them "buy" CSELC. The sale was effected by letting the seller
retain 270 of the agreements for deed and CSELC retained
the other 500. The monthly income on those 500 agreements
was essentially all the income CSELC had and they were, for
practical purposes, its only asset. Had the lot purchasers known

the financial condition of CSELC they would have known that ever receiving clear title to their lot was not going to happen.

It didn't. Even though the Division of Land Sales (DLS) of the State of Florida had assumed jurisdiction to police the development it was having no success in corralling the deceptive Sidney Jaffe. He was using his corporations, his *alter egos,* to funnel the lot payments into bank accounts over which he had total control and they became his personal funds. His machinations included institution of a "cash up" program promising a discount on the purchase price for an early payoff. Twenty-seven people opted for the cash up and received *quit claim* deeds which were absolutely worthless.

In early 1978 Barbara Raymond and other investors filed suit against CSELC to set aside various transfers and recover their money. Jaffe shortly responded by having CSELC file for bankruptcy in California. That claim (bankruptcy) was then moved to Florida and resulted in the appointment of a trustee who also became the receiver in the Barbara Raymond action. Jaffe then filed a series of frivolous lawsuits in both federal and state courts. He frivolously defended the Raymond action and never made a meaningful account of the lot payments ordered by the bankruptcy court.

DLS finally asked for my assistance. I assigned the case to Special Prosecutions and Glenn Norris was assigned the investigation. He did an exceptional job and we filed an information alleging land sale violations on the issuance of the twenty-eight *quit claim* deeds. These deeds were absolutely worthless.

Sydney Jaffe was arrested, arraigned in Putnam County and posted a bond of $135,000. On the application for the bail bond he listed a California address as his residence and the bond was conditioned that he not move from that address without the permission of the bail bond company. Having posted the bond, he went directly to his condominium in Toronto, Ontario.

On May 18, 1981 he failed to appear for trial. His defense attorney had sought a continuance of the trial on grounds that Jaffe, for medical reasons, had been rendered unable to travel. We later learned that on the trial date Jaffe and his wife were traveling in Europe. The bail bond was estreated and a *capias* issued. During a subsequent hearing the estreature was set aside on the condition that the bail bond company put $137,500 in escrow and have Jaffe before the court in ninety days. Sometime during this time frame we had our second request for extradition denied by the U.S. Secretary of State because the offenses charged were not extraditable under the treaty between the United States and Canada.

The bail bond company hired two bounty hunters and they, posing as policemen, retrieved Jaffe from his Toronto condominium and deposited him in the Putnam County jail. He was tried on the land sale counts and the failure to appear and was convicted on all. His sentencing was set for February 11, 1982.

Shortly prior to sentencing I received a letter and calls from a Deputy Assistant Legal Advisor (DALA) to the Secretary of State of the United States of America. The DALA requested that I delay the sentencing partly because "...the Department of State and the U.S. Justice Department were of the view that a Canadian protest contained allegations that raised serious questions of international law which the departments wished to discuss further with the appropriate Florida authorities...". The allegations were as follows:

On or about the 6th day of November 1981, the Cana-

dian embassy in Washington, acting on the instructions of
the Canadian authorities in Ottawa, lodged an official protest with the United States Department of State express-
ing their concern over the manner in which Mr. Sidney Jaffe
was kidnapped from Canada and requesting that the United
States authorities arrange for the present court proceedings instituted against Sidney Jaffe be stayed or quashed
and that Sidney Jaffe be released and returned to Canada.

The request was a strange one in that the Kerr-Frisbee
doctrine was no longer seriously contested. It stood for the
proposition that our courts (state and federal) did not have to
consider the circumstances which brought a fugitive into their
jurisdiction. Because of it agents, yes even agents of the requesting justice department, sometimes captured fugitives on
foreign soil and flew them to a federal facility to await trial.

The conversation, including its tone and content, made
me believe that the legal advisor surely thought that he was
conversing with a simple piney woods prosecutor who would
easily be intimidated. I refused the request and he entreated
me to reconsider since he was acting for and under the direction of the Secretary of State. I refused to reconsider and simply hung up.

Jaffe was sentenced to 145 years, but because some sentences were concurrent the sentence amounted to only 35
years. He was transported to prison during February, 1982.

On March 3, 1983 I was called by a parole commissioner
and informed that the Parole Commission, on March 2, 1983,
had reconsidered Jaffe's Presumptive Parole Release Date
(PPRD) and set it for May 24, 1983. On March 4, 1983 I
called the Commission and was referred to Commissioner
Simmons. I got no good answers concerning their action.

I did my research and found that Jaffe's PPRD had not
been on the March 2 agenda which was a serious violation of

procedure. Notwithstanding the agenda absence, Jaffe's wife and lawyer were present as was a Mr. Cole, who was Director of the Legal Advisory Commission of the Department of External Affairs in Ottawa, Canada. It, according to a tape of the proceeding, was a love-in. Nobody was there in opposition because of the apparent secrecy surrounding the meeting.

Florida Attorney General Jim Smith and I filed a petition for a Writ of *Certiorari* in the First District Court of Appeals alleging that the Commission's action was a deviation from the essential requirements of law. The Court found it to be so and indicated the deviation was compounded by the fact that the agenda failed to mention Jaffe. The Commission action was quashed.

Following my conversation with the State Department Legal Advisor, I and my participating staff members had been thoroughly investigated by the "appropriate Florida authorities" on the allegations that we aided and abetted the bounty hunters. The investigation concluded that there was no evidence to support the allegations.

On May 24, 1983 the Commission reconvened to consider Jaffe's release from prison. Mr. Cole again addressed the Commission concerning my "complicity" with the bounty hunters. His statements concerning that subject matter were as follows:

> After many months of discussions with the U.S. State and Justice Departments, The U.S. Department of Justice in November 1982 acknowledged their obligation and their authority to intervene in the Jaffe case if the facts so warrant. I might explain that under international law, the United States government is responsible for the wrongful act of the State of Florida, one of its constituent units.
> There then followed some six months of discussions with the U.S. Department of Justice off and on concerning

the investigation into the case that had been requested by the government. . .that had been requested of the government of Florida by the United States Attorney General, Mr. William French Smith.

At one point we were informed that the investigation would be completed by mid April, but we understand that the investigation—the report of the investigation has as yet not been completed.

In these circumstances, it is a matter of vital importance to the Canadian government that Mr. Jaffe, the victim of this shocking, illegal, and inhumane incident, should be returned to Canada at the earliest possible moment. The Canadian government is considering all the options that may be open to it with a view to realizing this objective.

My rebuttal was brief but I believed it totally undermined Mr. Cole's position. It was as follows:

MR. BOYLES: My presentation should be within ten minutes. . . I would like to respond first to the last person that was before the commission, Mr. Cole with the Department of External Affairs, as I understand it, and the proposition that he was raising before the commission.

There is a letter before the commission that was filed by the inmate Sydney Jaffe which came from the Department of External Affairs, I presume the department that he was with, and was addressed to a Mr. Sidney Framm, who was an attorney for Mr. Jaffe. That letter was written by the Department of External Affairs of Canada the day before they lodged their protest note to the American State Department.

And in there they said in that letter to Mr. Framm that they had no bona fide evidence of state action in this case and, consequently, that they were going to forward a letter to the State Department of the United States on humanitarian grounds. And I'm looking for that letter at the moment, but it is in your file.

> Nothing has changed in that matter since that time, and unless Mr. Cole wants to presume under international law or Canadian law or United States law that there is somebody involved in the state action and wants to presume them guilty prior to that time they've been properly accused and tried—that's not the way we do it in Putnam County. We normally give the person accused of a crime a fair trial and they're not tried in the papers.
>
> But, be that as it may, I think you ought to look at that letter where the Department of External Affairs, on the day before they lodged that protest, said they had no bona fide evidence, and they still don't have any bone fide evidence because it doesn't exist.

On July 8, 1983, realizing once again that I was before a hostile forum in the form of the Parole Commission, I filed an Organized Fraud charge against Sidney Jaffe. It was based on his receipt of purchaser payments after he had been court ordered to turn these monies over to the trustee/receiver. His bond was set at $150,000..

During late July 1983 William French Smith, U.S. Attorney General and George Shultz, Secretary of State, filed a request to appear at an upcoming Commission meeting to be heard in favor of moving up Jaffe's PPRD. The Secretary personally signed his request and it included an assertion that "...the United States has an extradition treaty with Canada. That treaty could have been utilized to secure Mr. Jaffe's return; no one has suggested the contrary...". He then wanted to know why our office made no other efforts for a legally sufficient extradition request. The innuendo was still there that we aided and abetted the bounty hunters.

These two departments were at best grossly mistaken and out of control. It was their departments that notified the Governor of Florida that Jaffe could not be extradited because the land sales offenses were not offenses extraditable under the treaty! Had their staff not informed them of such?

On this or another occasion the Secretary of State had indicated to the Commission that while there was no "credible" evidence of my complicity with the bounty hunters the Canadians believed it to be so and Jaffe should therefore be paroled. The use of the term "credible" I suspected was to conjure up the notion that where there's smoke there's fire.

On September 29, 1983 the land sale convictions were reversed in an opinion that I still do not understand. I had to concede that if what we proved to the jury was not sufficient for a conviction the land sales legislation was essentially absent any viable criminal sanctions.

Jaffe was shortly paroled to the detainer (the Organized Fraud charge), posted bail and returned to Canada. During that hearing I was a lonely figure in opposition. The failure-to-appear conviction was not overturned and my argument basically was that conviction and the restitution to only twenty-seven of 500 victims warranted his continued incarceration. The next day, while in my Daytona office, I received separate calls from two Parole Board commissioners suggesting that I had really made my case and that Jaffe deserved incarceration for the rest of his life. When I asked why they had voted for parole the phone went silent.

The Jaffe case, for several years, had produced substantial headlines in many newspapers across the U.S. and Canada. Dr. Joseph France, the happy hour friend, was at one time in a medical conference in Los Angeles and in the largest paper there he read front page news about the Citra frog hunter. It was my reply to a newspaper reporter concerning my position on the parole since the Secretary of State was firmly and personally its strong advocate. My simple reply was that I did not presume to tell the Secretary how to run his shop and

I was disinclined to listen to his suggestions on how I should run mine.

Sidney Jaffe was doubtless an extremely intelligent man but after returning to Canada he lent great credence to the old adage that "A lawyer who represents himself has a fool for a client." During 1985 he and his wife, representing themselves, filed a suit in a Canadian court naming over twenty people or entities as defendants. The suit style was *Sidney L. Jaffe, et.ux.vs Joe C. Miller,II,et.al.,* Ontario Court of Justice, case # 85-CQ-6103. I and several of my staff were included as defendants as was the trustee/receiver to the Florida bankruptcy court. The claim was for ten million dollars and those were said to be the damages he suffered as a result of the "conspiracy" against him and his wife. The trustee/receiver counter-claimed to enforce a three million dollar judgment he had won against Jaffe in a Florida Federal Court.

The Canadian judge, in 1994, rendered judgment against the Jaffes and for the trustee/receiver. Pursuant to the judgment their condominium was sold and most of the lot purchasers received five to ten cents on the dollar for their losses. I and my staff had earlier on been dismissed from the suit because of sovereign immunity.

The findings by the judge, which preceded the judgment, poignantly exposed Jaffe as an evil, wicked and twisted man. The findings also vindicated our actions in the Jaffe saga and in my view, in so doing, they revealed the sham advocacy of the highly placed public officials who parroted Jaffe's accusations. Some of the most pertinent findings were as follows:

....

Something much more than conversation between individuals is required to have them involved in a conspiracy. This is especially so when, as here, there has always existed very valid reasons for. . . Boyles and others to be in touch with each other and to exchange information. One group was pursuing Jaffe in civil proceedings while others were interested in criminal proceedings. There is nothing in the evidence to support Jaffe's claim that those on the civil side used the criminal processes to attempt to extract money from Jaffe or the corporations.

....

In my opinion, there is simply no evidence that permits a conclusion that there was any conspiracy of any kind on the part of the defendants, whether it be those who remain in the action, those who have been let out, or those ... against whom Jaffe did not proceed, with respect to the kidnapping, or any of the land sales charges, the organized fraud charges or the perjury charges. And I must reach the same conclusion about the alleged mistreatment while Jaffe was a prisoner in the Putnam County jail.

....

Had Jaffe not caused himself to be regarded as a fugitive from justice at the time of his being kidnapped, virtually nothing of what occurred thereafter would have arisen. I think it is only reasonable to suggest that everything that did happen to him once he left Canada was due to his own misconduct. In my view, he was not wrongfully imprisoned in the Putnam County Jail following the kidnapping. I find it difficult to accept that Jaffe can be considered to have been damnified by doing what he was otherwise legally compelled to do. As well, in my view, the actions of Kear and Johnsen in kidnapping Jaffe represent the *causa sine qua non* while Jaffe's own conduct is the *causa causans* of what transpired after Jaffe crossed the border.

Concerning Mrs. Jaffe:

On some occasions this concern on her part pushed her to the ridiculous. For instance, she was asked during cross-examination whether she had traveled to Europe with Jaffe on a vacation during the summer of 1981. She was obviously taken back by this question because she knew that Jaffe's excuse for not appearing in Florida to deal with the land sales charges in May or attending a civil hearing in August was that an injury had prevented him from traveling. With some hesitation, Mrs. Jaffe replied that she was not sure if Jaffe had accompanied her to Europe that summer. For his part, when asked later, Jaffe had no difficulty admitting that he had in fact accompanied Mrs. Jaffe to Europe in the summer of 1981. He also said with no hesitation, "Going on vacation is one thing, being examined is another."

....

Insofar as Jaffe's credibility is concerned, I can say without hesitation that in all my years on the Bench, I have not seen or experienced a more untrustworthy witness or litigant. Jaffe absolutely has no compunction about any kind of misconduct whether his or that of others whom he has asked to act in his interest. It is so obvious that falsehood and deception forms part of most, if not everything, he does that I cannot understand how intelligent people, such as Mrs. Jaffe, his friend and associate Alter, and his long-time lawyer Zeldin, have found it necessary to go as far as each has gone in support of his conduct.

....

It appears to me that central to everything that Jaffe has said or done or caused to be said or done since 1976 is his steadfast refusal to account for the money which he caused to be collected from St. Johns [the development] between 1976 and 1982. I believe that he commenced this action primarily as a means of permitting the situation to continue. As it now stands he has succeeded in having another nine years go by without having to account for what was taken or to produce documents or records from which anyone else can reach a conclusion. He does not deny that money was taken; he simply does not want anyone to find out how much.

....

My immediate reaction upon the completion of the trial was that nine years, of which ten weeks were spent at trial, has been consumed indulging Jaffe and his use of the court's processes to further an ulterior motive. Jaffe has been able to mask his real intention by generating an air of legitimacy to this action by his kidnapping and his discharge of the land sales charges. Unfortunately, without going through this whole trial, the fact that the die had been cast long before either of those two events occurred could not be known in my opinion. There is absolutely no justification whatsoever for this action, let alone this trial, having taken place.

This judge, surely a true jurist, made his findings and conclusions based on the evidence presented by the parties to the suit. That evidence and much more of a related nature were available to the Attorney General and the Secretary of State while they were parroting the Jaffe distortions before the Parole Commission.

Vindication, for me and my staff, was a long time coming but it came very sweetly flavored. Sydney Jaffe is still a fugitive from justice in Florida.

26

Acute myocardial infarction and defeat as SA

My unopposed election in the fall of 1984 was rapidly followed by an acute myocardial infarction (AMI) of the lower right ventricle. Over the years I had developed a squad of handball players and games usually included three or four players. Two were singles and four were doubles. Three was "cutthroat", the server playing against the other two.

In mid to late January, 1985 we had a doubles going for about two and a half hours. We were playing outdoors in thirties degree weather with a light misty rain. Bill Townsend arrived and I played singles with him while the others played cutthroat and the single lasted one and a half to two hours.

I left in the family van which had become necessary because of the size of the family and I remember Bill Townsend saying, "You sure you're alright?" My reply was, "Sure, just tired."

I drove about 10 blocks and decided that the exhaustion, with the weather, had created a chill. I pulled over and parked on St. Johns Avenue. I lay down and pulled my jacket over me to chase away the chill but a nagging pressure across the back of my shoulders increased in intensity. It would not allow rest. It didn't seem to work and I drove to the emergency room, not really knowing why. I went to the reception desk, still in sweaty clothing, and the receptionist needed my insurance card. I replied that it was in my brief case in the van which was in the parking lot. She took a second look and replied, "Never mind, please come with me" and I was escorted in.

I remembered being on a bed and the doctor asking how I felt on a scale of one to ten. Miss Sara was there at that point but I did not remember how she was notified. I responded, "About a three or four". I later learned that my blood pressure was then sixty over thirty instead of my normal one hundred twelve over seventy (when I was excited). The next thing I remembered was being in intensive care and a nurse was having great difficulty in removing a jock strap from my tired and sweaty body. I told her to cut it off and it was done. I remembered little about the next nine days because of the medication. I did remember Dr. Joseph M. France, Jr. paying what he thought were "last respects" to his close friend. Others told me about their visits but I remembered little.

I was released to go home and arranged another cardiac catheterization at North Florida. On the way out we met the head nurse, a friend of the family, and she wanted to know if Miss Sara had the prescription for the needed medication. Miss Sara responded yes that Dr. Weigel had written all my prescriptions. Pat Baxter said, "No, no, *your* prescription, Sally--you are about to be home-bound with an obsessive/compulsive fifty-year-old for six weeks!" She was right. The only thing saving her sanity would be books, books, books, CNN and sedatives which produced my naps. I had weekly meetings with the Division Chiefs on the porch and we set up non-emergency calling times. Emergencies would permit calls at any time. I probably understood that stress had taken its toll but I was still on my "watch". If the train jumped the track I was the engineer.

I had the second cardiac catheterization and learned that all other heart arteries and veins were better than normal for a man my age.

I returned to work. The real side effect for an AMI was that for several years thereafter almost all normal aches and pains were an indicator that the second heart attack was on its way.

I tried to normalize my life by returning to handball but it didn't work. It made my comrades nervous and I played at about eighty-five percent speed to avoid the second AMI. An obsessive/compulsive can't play at eighty-five percent without great frustration. My handball days were over but the unpadded gloves remained in my dresser drawer. They would only be a memento. No pads were needed because the hands were tough. They had wielded hammers, axes and post hole diggers.

The years of the new term were almost exclusively administrative. It was budget, personnel, interviews with applicants and annual sessions with all employees concerning performance reports. The sessions lasted about two hours and there were more than one hundred employees. They were conducted in the office where the employee worked. The evenings still included the press calls, usually at supper time. The Governor knew of my AMI — it had been widely reported —and he reduced my special assignments to avoid unnecessary stress.

My central office had been moved to Bunnell, which, geographically, was about the center of the circuit. I spent the mornings there and then drove to Daytona. Bunnell was only about twenty minutes from home and it provided the shortest drive for any meeting with a Division Chief. It also provided me a shorter drive and worked well for regular Division Chief meetings.

During sometime early in 1988 John Tanner (a former ASA of mine) visited me in the Bunnell office and explained that he would be running for State Attorney. John had been hired by my predecessor and I kept him on as an assistant. He had been a Division Chief early on but had entered private practice doing mostly criminal defense work. He had been an able advocate from either chair. He had heard that I had been "sick" and he loved me like a brother and Miss Sara like a sister. But he must do what a man was called to do.

Another campaign was under way but I had first to attend to Leslie's wedding. She had been dating "Moochie" — Daniel Eugene Wilkinson — who was the drummer in the David Burkhalter and the Wilkinson Brothers Band. He drove a red van, had a daughter (Brandy)by a prior marriage,and like all parents, we did not at first think he was suitable to marry our first-born daughter. His first visit to the house had produced a dog bite from SLB, Jr's leopard cur and that surely meant he had no place in our family. "Moochie" had exited the van in the back yard and was patting the friendly tail-wagging cur all the way to the back door. The knock on the back door would draw blood from his ankle. He was too close to the children whom the leopard dog protected from all human harm. Moochie became a super son-in-law, and Brandy became our grandaughter.

Leslie graduated from Santa Fe in Gainesville and had a degree in oral hygiene. She passed the state test and became employed. We had bought her a new car on her sixteenth birthday, a bad precedent considering there were three more to come.

I did not know we were soon to be in a classic father-of-the-bride situation. My first suggestion was to have my friends do the barbecue in the back yard but that was rejected out of hand. All my other suggestions received a smile and "I don't think so". The reception was to be at home, be catered and a giant tent would cover the tables, dance floor, and live band. It was a total success in hospitality but it had cost maybe fifteen times what I expected to spend. About mid-way through the plans for the second wedding reception (Allyson's) I would learn a rule that made such things go much more smoothly: Simply sign the checks and keep your mouth shut. I saw "Father of the Bride" and almost did not recover from the belly laughs.

The lack of handball had added twelve pounds to a weaker heart. I knew that doing my job was accumulating defendants and their families as enemies every day. I knew that there were law enforcement officers (LEO's) dissatisfied with our charging policy but I didn't know how many. Finally, I knew that the circuit was becoming more and more Republican. The 1988 campaign would soon be underway and when it started Leslie wanted to know when I would kick into the ole "kick butt and take names later" mode. That mode probably never got going over eighty-five percent of its original but it really didn't matter. There was a Republican landslide to include the ouster of myself, the next Speaker of the Florida House of Representatives (who was from Daytona), and a many-term popular Congressman whose district was very similar to my circuit. John Tanner was elected.

We were at the house of John Doyle, an Assistant State Attorney Division Chief, when we learned it was over. We left, stopped by the *Daytona Beach News Journal* office and thanked Ms. Davidson for all her efforts. We drove home and the Putnam faithful were still there but it was a rather subdued "election" party. It had been a sad day but I would later learn it produced a tomorrow far superior to what the election would have provided. I had become sorely stressed by the enormity and complexity of a twenty-eight year caseload of tall proportions. The stress was enhanced by being desk-bound. It had been time for a change. I was only then mature enough (at age fifty-four) to concede, privately and publicly, that a toll had been taken. But it was my fault for not having sat regularly alone atop a north Georgia mountain.

The next morning the *News Journal* called, and I simply responded that it was the people's office and the people had spoken and that I would soon appoint Mr. Tanner a Special Assistant in order that he might become familiar with budget and administrative matters prior to taking over. Four years later the transition would not be so smooth.

27

SLB elected circuit judge; some selected cases

The far superior "tomorrow" did have a slow start. I had no job and no income except retirement pay. Stephen and Allyson were both in college at the University of Florida and Dell would soon be attending Vanderbilt. I had under construction a cabin in Hiawassee, Georgia. A recent inheritance, withdrawal of my deferred compensation and sale of the cabin would tide me over and allow purchase of all that was needed for a law office. I had opted early retirement as State Attorney because of medical insurance costs. The time between the election and opening of the Bunnell law office was a very welcome respite. It was a true sabbatical. I made many trips to Hiawassee to attend to cabin building and my brother-in-law quarters were provided by the other twin and her husband. They had moved permanently to Hiawassee and had a home atop a mountain overlooking Lake Chatuge. The view was breathtaking but soothing. My soul was renourished and my energy was refueled.

Friends and family were now saying, "You look ten years younger!" I felt ten years younger! That would make my appearance age forty-four and my actual age fifty-four. I started practicing in Bunnell and did criminal defense in all four counties. I also did probate and real estate. My secretary was Kathy

Dees, the wife of former Division Chief Jeffrey L. Dees. Jeff was then an Assistant US Attorney in Orlando. It was not to his liking and we became partners and opened another office in Daytona. Judge Eastmoore was known to be talking about retirement as a Circuit Judge sitting mostly in Palatka and I began to think about running and asked Jeff's views.

I had hired Jeff upon his graduation from Harvard Law School. These two ex-prosecutors defended a Murder One case in the Palatka Courthouse where I had begun my duties as Assistant State Attorney. I was in the first chair and Jeff was feeding me ammunition. I did my closing argument without notes and began to slowly dissect the prosecution's "evidence." I then warmed into the prosecution's theory of the case which by its own evidence excluded the defendant having been in a place, and at an angle, to have been the shooter. I explained it in some detail. It unraveled their case and the Assistant State Attorney's mind. I noted from the corner of my eye that he was in pain and wanted to apologize for having "brought" the case. He didn't have to. When the verdict was announced the foreman simply explained that it was a case that should never have been brought.

My charging policies had obviously been loosened if not emasculated. After my argument Jeff had said, "Why would you want to become a Judge and waste all that talent?". I was beginning to believe the answer might be to commute five miles per day instead of fifty and for some reason I remembered General Tibbits addressing me as "Judge."

Miss Sara didn't object to this career change. She was absolutely for it but was I up to another campaign? I explained this one was non-partisan and Court Canons greatly restricted how a Judge could campaign. A candidate could not even attend an affair sponsored by a political party except under rare circumstances. Besides, my energy had been refueled. Mr. Tanner was receiving bad press and many supporters sensed an air of "atonement" for the past election.

My only opponent was from Palatka and he was as mild-mannered as I. He greatly outspent me but it didn't overcome all the supporters I had gained over the years. According to the press I "rolled" to victory. My opponent was later appointed to replace another Judge and we became good friends. We were and had been in the same church. I was sworn in, invested, and attended two required courses for new judges in Tallahassee. They were put on by the Florida Judicial College. On my second return Joseph M. France, Jr. was on the porch with Miss Sara to constitute a two-person homecoming committee. I was relaxed and looking forward to the next tour.

I replaced Judge Eastmoore and Judge Robert Perry was his replacement as Chief Administrative Judge for Putnam County. He answered to the Chief Judge of the Circuit. The only other judge in the Courthouse was County Judge Peter T. Miller. We had a visiting Circuit Judge who, on a part-time basis, handled juvenile delinquency and dependency matters. Judge Perry and I did fifty percent each of every Circuit Court case filed. Circuit Court jurisdiction included domestic relations (simplified dissolution, dissolution, child support, domestic violence and other domestic relations), torts, professional malpractice, products liability, auto negligence and other negligence and other civil matters including contracts, condominium, eminent domain and real property/mortgage foreclosures. It also included jurisdiction over all felony criminal cases.

Our calendars included two jury panels per month for jury trials. The week I calendared for criminal trials he calendared

for civil trials and we backed each other up. The other weeks
were usually in chambers involving the "equity" side of our
jurisdiction which was mostly non-jury. Those cases involved
the Judge as fact-finder and Judge and they were usually called
bench trials. A bench trial for most Judges was far more de-
manding than a jury trial. The judge was also the "jury".

Judge Perry had been an ole warhorse trial lawyer. We
had clashed several times following the tradition of leaving
the courtroom battles in the courtroom. He had been on the
campaign trail running for Circuit Judge during a time I was
running for re-election as State Attorney. He would occasionally, when he had an audience, mock my usual beginning statements in a campaign speech. It went like this: "Ladies and
Gentlemen, it has been a high, *high* honor for me to have
served you these past years as your State Attorney. But I know
that my tenure depends on whether I have done the right thing
in the right way. I know, and hope you believe, that I have
never prosecuted or failed to prosecute because of fear, favor,
or hope of reward. . ." It was true. It might have been a little
flowery but I had no capacity to mask insincerity. I knew he
liked it and I suspected that when we were not on the same
platform he might borrow some words.

Our general jurisdiction was rapidly becoming a thing of
the past. Most Judges were sitting in specialized divisions
where they heard only family law cases, juvenile cases, civil
jury cases, criminal cases, or some other.

I rapidly discovered that my constant companion was my
calendar which was set a year in advance. I dug in, and jury
or non-jury, resolved thousands of cases. I tried with a jury
about forty criminal cases a year and they included murder,
rape, robbery, burglary and numerous property crimes.

One murder case appeared interesting and I invited Joseph M. France, Sr. and his wife Vera, the parents of my close friend, to observe. We dined in chambers during lunch time. The case took three or four days. The defendant and his then-wife had a domestic quarrel about five years prior to this trial. The defendant had broken the glass of the front door of their home with "brass knucks" which he had made from an auto transmission part. They weighed about 2 lbs. The wife had stabbed his eye out with a shard of the glass. The Sheriff's Office had investigated and sometime later seized the knucks only to place them subsequently on a shelf not in the evidence locker.

Sometime later the defendant was seen leaving a bar with his girlfriend on a specific date. She was missing for five years before her skeleton was found and examined. A forensic anthropologist from the University of Florida did the examination. He was called in after the cause of death was "established" as a skull fracture. Somehow the "knucks" were sent to him and he opined that they were consistent with the skull fracture. On the stand he testified that further examination made him conclude they were the murder weapon. The skull was in evidence and from the witness stand he demonstrated the match. The defendant was convicted and sentenced to life in prison. An appeal was filed and the Appellate Court affirmed the conviction. The Frances saw "justice" in a real-life setting.

Another criminal case involved a co-ed returning to the University of Florida via Palatka on a Sunday afternoon. She was at the McDonald's drive-thru and a gunman forced her to the passenger side and drove to Miami. On the way she was raped and sodomized about seven times. She was deposited on the street and while making a 911 call at a pay telephone her watch was snatched from her arm. The abductor was caught, prosecuted and chose to make his own closing argument. The prosecutor almost stepped over the line in his closing argument and I had to take an unusual step of reigning him in. The defendant, then representing himself, didn't know how to object. It could have caused a conviction reversal. The defendant was convicted and I sentenced him to a number of years which would result in life imprisonment.

Civil cases included automobile and boating personal injury cases tried before a jury. Some other jury cases included contracts involving both real and personal property and products liability cases. One such case involved a death and serious injury alleged to have been caused by "a lift kit" which raised the center of gravity and the height of pick-up trucks. The plaintiff's theory was that the "after-market" kit had caused a roll-over which resulted in the death and injury. The case involved two well-matched lawyers having way above excellent skills. Every "quirk" which can occur in a jury trial occurred. On the morning before final arguments we learned there had been a TV segment on the dangers of such lift kits. The defendant's lawyer wanted to poll the jury to see if any had watched and the plaintiff's attorney was opposed. I finally decided on the poll and one juror had seen the show but had not discussed it with his fellow jurors. I asked if we could agree to excuse him in favor of the alternate juror? The defendant, not the plaintiff, objected! I excused the juror, final arguments were made, and I instructed the jury. They came back with a verdict and my examination revealed the three million dollar or so verdict had to be a miscalculation. At benchside we agreed to send them back pointing out the discrepancy. The verdict was later overturned because of an unobjected-to remark in the plaintiff's lawyer's closing argument. The plaintiff appealed to the Supreme Court and the matter was settled while the appeal was pending.

These examples don't include the countless hours and cases trying to resolve dissolutions of marriage and child custody. Those matters involved the judge having to decide who got what and who was the primary custodial parent of the children. Those matters included both sides trying to *"pro se"* (without lawyer) change the judgment in post judgment actions. Those *pro se* actions made for a perfect schism in the law concerning access to the courts and no *ex parte* access to the judge. They would try a judge's soul and my position was, and still is, that a judge should not hear only such matters for eight hours every day for eighteen months.

I should note that we were rapidly approaching a caseload justifying three circuit judges and the same caseload divided by three instead of two would make a world of difference.

That time had not arrived when the Phimmachack case happened.

28

Tries without jury a defendant charged with murdering five people

Kingkhamvong Phimmachack was a Laotian refugee who fled Laos during the early seventies civil war. His real name was Phim-sipasom, but he assumed the name of the family he connected with in a Thailand refugee camp while fleeing. He arrived in the U.S. and settled in with his adoptive family in a small town in South Carolina. He was then in his teens and his residency in South Carolina included only an arrest for a DUI which resulted in some injuries to others.

He moved to Lake Como in South Putnam County and obtained a job with Millers Ice Company in Crescent City. He married a local girl and they took up residency in Lake Como. They became parents of three girls and the maternal grandmother became the primary day-time caretaker.

On April 3, 1995 probably around 9:30 p.m., the mother-in-law, wife and three children were systematically gunned down in their home. The wife and one child were killed in the master bedroom, two children were killed in a smaller bedroom and the mother-in-law was killed in the kitchen. Phimmachack then shot himself in the chest but, miraculously, survived.

The press — local, state and national — had become consumed with the case. Phimmachack became a defendant, and the case for me became time-consuming and pre-trial hearings were reported in every detail. One *Palatka Daily News* editorial chastised me severely for allowing Patrick Canan (specially assigned defense counsel) to travel to Laos to investigate the background of his client to further what would be an insanity defense. The paper said it was a colossal waste of taxpayer money.

The *Palatka Daily News* didn't know, but I did, that collateral attacks on death penalty convictions and many other lesser cases were focused on the Sixth Amendment right-to-counsel issues and the thrust of such actions was to vacate a judgment and sentence because the defendant's counsel had rendered "ineffective assistance of counsel." In Florida they were called "3.850s" — the number of the Supreme Court rule which adopted and governed their filing. Denial of the trip, without doubt, would have been the centerpiece of a 3.850 brought in this case if a conviction was affirmed on appeal. It did and it was. The writer of the *Daily News* editorial was about two steps behind, but that was a short distance for most of his opinions on criminal justice.

The pretrial was over and on motion and because of massive local publicity I changed the *venue* to Daytona Beach and jury selection began in November, 1996. Selection was not going well as both prosecutors and defenders were getting off the wall answers concerning prospective juror views on the insanity defense and imposition of the death penalty. We all knew, again because of the publicity, that the jury would have to be sequestered from day one. That alone was risky business because only one juror reading publicity about the trial would be grounds for mistrial. Logistics of such sequestering was also a massive undertaking. I knew that both counsel were among the best in the business and that they were very able, thorough, talented and civil. That would make the trial itself easy to preside over. Seated at second chair for the defense was one Robert L. McLeod, Jr., a former Division Chief of mine, and it was rumored that he believed himself equally as talented as, if not more talented than, the Citra lawyer. He and his partner, Patrick Canan, were truly talented and true professionals. The prosecution team was John Stephenson and Garry Wood. They regularly prosecuted in my division and I knew they were of the same caliber.

The prospective juror answers hatched a conspiracy. Both sides wondered whether a truly fair, informed and unbiased jury could be seated to resolve the issues at hand. Both sides knew the Judge to be an experienced prosecutor and defender, a man of many life experiences who was in fact tough but always fair even if fair meant taking considerable heat. The judge was an ex-prosecutor who believed that the Fourth Amendment had to be adhered to even if it brought down considerable criticism by lazy or overzealous police officers which could not ethically be responded to by a judge. Post trial press interviews with all the participating lawyers verified this seemingly self-serving and immodest account.

During midafternoon of the third day, and following a break, both sides announced they were waiving a jury trial. It was like being hit in the temple, at close range, with a cannon ball. It knocked me off my feet but my hard head resisted further injury.

I remember Patrick Canan saying, with true concern, "Judge, do you want to do it this way?" and I simply responded, "I'm a company man, and this is what they pay me for." I was secretly wondering if American life was askew. We paid athletes hundreds of thousands per month and we paid the ones who decided life and death a little over $100,000 *per year.* I could see that all the advocates had the experience to observe that a witness, opponent or Judge would reveal his thoughts, as opposed to his words, by eye contact, facial expression, demeanor or bearing. Knowing his true mind-set, they were able to deal with his words. How many times, with witnesses and opponents, had I enjoyed this advantage! But I also knew that the waiver of jury was made because they knew SLB would not shirk a duty. I considered the waiver to be both a compliment and a true burden. The trial began. I "comforted" myself with the knowledge that jury logistics would no longer be my concern. There were, however, other logistics to be dealt with.

The cowboy son-in-law named Dennis, the groom who had done his wedding dance with Corrine Adele on my pool deck, had convinced me to buy four full-blooded Limousin cows weighing about 1400 lbs each. They were "parked" in a two-thirds of an acre fenced enclosure which was part of our ample backyard. They each required about 40 pounds of hay per day and that required feeding two bales in the morning and two bales in the afternoon. Before sun up of each day of the trial I walked the gauntlet to deposit the hay in the hopper. One misstep and I would be trampled or at least suffer a broken foot. It became a joke at the trial about who took credit for the Court of a one-man jury having to feed up after dark.

The trial was no joke. The prosecution methodically put on its case and among other rulings, I as the Court had to rule on whether the photographs of the death scene were too inflammatory for me as the jury to see. My ruling required that I see the photographs to determine if they were admissible for me to see.

I suspected that most, if not all, Judges would have "talked" the lawyers out of a jury waiver in such a case. Soon, when the State rested its case, I would have to rule on a motion for judgment of acquittal (JOA). That required a determination of whether the evidence was sufficient, taking all inferences in favor of the State, to support a verdict of 'guilty' by a reasonable jury. I knew of no other case in the country where a bench trial had occurred on a capital case of this severity and this one was receiving national publicity each day.

The motion for JOA was denied and the defense put on the insanity defense. It was mostly experts who then had, as a result of the Laos trip, the childhood experiences of the defendant including his witnessing of classmates being gunned down by the soldiers of the warring factions. The father of Kingkhamvong Phimmachak testified and the interpreter, from the University of Florida, broke under the stress and heartache. He couldn't go on and had to be replaced. He had witnessed a reunion of father and son during a noon recess. I later learned that hardened bailiffs, monitoring the reunion, had openly wept. I also later learned that Patrick Canan had kept photos of his children in his briefcase to avoid becoming "unglued."

Closing arguments were made; the defendant had "lost it" during his lawyer's argument and that was his first and only show of emotion. I took the jury instructions to the jury room which had a table and twelve chairs. Only one chair would be needed. Eleven were hauntingly empty. The "jury" discovered a mistake in the jury instructions and reconvened the Court. Now as Judge he learned that the advocates agreed, and the instruction was corrected. I re-entered the jury room and was immediately transformed into the "jury."

I recessed for the evening with an agreement that, surviving the hay feed, I would continue my deliberations while sequestered on my porch. Miss Sara could observe from the family room but not violate the sequester. The following morning, with little sleep, I returned to the jury room. I realized that I owed the legal warriors more than a verdict form which simply provided for a checkmark in the 'guilty' or 'not guilty' line. I prepared my findings on a yellow pad. They were in hand print but have been reproduced in type because of the poor quality of the copy. They were as follows:

ORDER OF DELIBERATIONS
1) Read instructions
2) Examined physical evid and exhibits
3) Found glitch in volunt intox instr
4) Reflected on testimony
5) Considered insanity defense

    A) Considered amok [i.e., how the defendant's traumatic childhood experiences during the civil war had damaged him] and how it relates to Florida's slightly modified McNaughton insanity — concluded that I could not rewrite the Florida insanity doctrine to include the elements of amok but that I could consider the elements of amok on the issues of "right from wrong."

    B) Reflected on the testimony of Dr. Krop and concluded that his testimony had less probative value than the other experts. I was bothered by the processes (sic?) involved in arriving at his opinion.

    C) Reflected on the testimony of Dr. Westermeyer--hard to imagine the existence of a professional with more superb credentials (in his field) than his. But listening to his testimony I found a lack of firmness in his opinion on the crucial issues. I found the "lack of an abiding conviction" that his opinion was well grounded.

    D) Reflected on the testimony of Dr. Green. I found his professional career to be remarkable for his age. At first blush I thought I detected a hint of arrogance. I finally concluded that the appearance of arrogance was really a reflection of the firmness and abiding character of his opinion. I concluded that his testimony was focused on the true issues, that it was the most straightforward of the experts and that it was the best reasoned in terms of how AMOK relates to our jurisprudence. I gave his testimony the greater weight.

E) Finally on the issue of insanity I considered pre and post episode actions and words of the defendant. I note here that I found the post episode statements to be voluntary (those that I considered). I note additionally that I remembered some of the prospective juror answers that "any man who kills his children has to be insane" and "I could never give credence to an insanity defense if it is proved that a man killed his children". I found the actions and words of the defendant to be inconsistent with legal insanity. I note, for example, that he expressed a clear conviction that the wife's conduct (perceived or real) was "wrong" and that the attempted suicide was (could be) self punishment for his wrongful conduct.

6) I conclude and find, beyond any reasonable doubt, that the defendant was not legally insane. Common sense convinces me that the defendant's state of mind, at the time of the killing, was jealous rage equating to unrestrained passion.

7) I note, perhaps out of order, that I find, beyond any reasonable doubt, that it was the defendant who shot, and killed, the victims named in the indictment.

8) On the issues of premeditation I find as follows:

A) Again using common sense I find the defendant's pre and post episode statements and actions to be inconsistent (with one exception) with the lack of a fully formed intent to kill. I find the order of the killing to be as argued by the prosecutor in closing argument. I find motive in the perceived infidelity. I find cognition and purpose from the time span required to complete the episode. I find the ejection of the dud bullets [shell casings], the loading/shooting, reloading/shooting, reloading/shooting and reloading/shooting to be inconsistent with any substantial alcohol impairment. My examination of the shotgun reveals a "stiff" breach and when fired and reloaded it automatically goes on safety (meaning that it has to be manually taken off before refiring). I finally add that the post episode telephone dialing and conversation refute any substantial impairment from alcohol. I believe that the actions required to complete this episode require far greater cognition than the rote/habit driving of an automobile.

The one exception is that the evidence on premeditation related to the victim Morrow [his mother-in-law]is less compelling. I do not recall (evidence of) her having been mentioned by the defendant in either pre or post episode statements. I have a reasonable doubt based on the evidence being consistent with her being killed simply because she obstructed (was in the way) to the other killings. There is no reasonable doubt that her killing meets the elements of murder in the second degree.

9) I conclude by completing and signing the judgment consistent with my findings.

11/27/96

Stephen L. Boyles (signature)

Court was reconvened and simply stating to Mr. Canan that I may have scarred his life with his special appointment as Public Defender, I added that I owed him more than a check on a form. I read my findings and entered the verdict.

I need to note here that the sister of the deceased mother had been "designated" to be the victim contact for all trial proceedings. She had been present at all pre-trial and trial proceedings and had been well-behaved. Not many family members losing kin to a homicide are. Most, but not all, are in an "eye for an eye" mode. I had been observing this observer and the eyes, bearing and demeanor gave no clue as to which mode she was in.

We reconvened for the penalty phase hearing and I heard the evidence on aggravators and mitigators. Florida law required that aggravators outweigh mitigators before the death penalty could be sustained. This was usually first determined by a jury under instructions by the Judge after hearing the evidence. They then made a recommendation but the ultimate decision on death or life imprisonment was for the Judge. Judges usually did follow the recommendations and almost no death penalties were upheld when the jury had recommended against. Once again I was "comforted" by not having to deal with the logistics of a jury in such a preceding.

During pre-trial and trial I was aware that the multiple-victim aggravator was present but the law did not permit death with only one aggravator. No other aggravator was at that time apparent unless the newly-enacted aggravator of victims being under twelve had been held to be applicable to murders occurring before the date of its enactment. The especially heinous and atrocious aggravator was not present because it was reserved for murders that included torture to the victim and a time span for the victim to suffer, knowing that death was coming.

I heard the evidence and the prosecution unconvincingly argued that their were two aggravators. I returned to the jury room and wrote my findings. They too have been typed for clarity. They read as follows:

12/18/96
Penalty Phase Deliberations
1) I read the instructions.
2) Reading the instructions I perceived that it would not be inappropriate to allow a "lay" consideration of the evidence and the instructions---a non lawyer/judge approach. Using this approach I found as follows:
    A) Beyond any doubt the previous conviction

aggravator was proven.

 B) The mitigators of no significant history of prior criminal activity, extreme mental or emotional disturbance, capacity substantially impaired, and all of the non-statutory mitigators (with the exception of traumatic brain injury) were proven using the reasonably convinced standard.

 3) Still using the "Steve Boyles" (citizen juror) approach I started the weighing process. I found the aggravator to be of great weight but that it would have been of greater weight if one of the prior convictions had occurred days, weeks, months or years prior to the episode. I found the mental capacity mitigators to about equal the aggravator in the case of the wife. Specifically I found that the jealousy, passion and rage somewhat mitigates the defendant's conduct of summarily accusing, trying and imposing the death penalty on the wife. But giving the defendant benefit of the balance "weighing" as to the wife there is no plausible pretense of this justification as to the children. I consider that in the lay definition of "heinous" there is no more heinous crime than unjustifiably killing children (though I am unable to conclude whether killing your own children is more wrong than killing stranger children).

 4) I opine that a lay jury would, by a majority vote, advise the death penalty.

 5) Now as judge I consider the recommendation and find as follows:

 A) I am both relieved and frustrated that I cannot impose the death penalty in this case. Relieved because no decent human being could ever enjoy such a task. I am frustrated because I believe that if this offense had occurred after October 1, 1995 the death penalty would be factually and legally justified. I, of course, refer to the new victim under twelve aggravator and refer you back to my lay thoughts on children killing. This factor with the other aggravator may well have outweighed the mitigators.

 I feel compelled to note an irony. I believe that most legal scholars would agree that Spinkelink's death penalty would not pass muster under current law (he was the first person electrocuted pursuant to Florida's post *Furman* capital case statute). The irony being that under current law imposition of the death penalty probably, in this case, would pass muster.

I should have noted before and do so now that the non use of the aggravator in this case was based on ex post facto grounds and while that issue has not been clearly and expressly ruled on I believe that its use in this case would have been reversed.

I close by noting that I realize my decision will be unpopular with the family in particular and Putnam Countians in general. I relate to and deeply sympathize with the gravity of the loss to the surviving family but I cannot, under my oath of office, let that sympathy obscure what I see as my clear duty. Finally I say to the family, if the defendant loved his family as he claims and as the evidence seems to support, his sentence, for him, may be worse than death — life in prison is hell on earth even without a conscience.

Stephen L. Boyles (signature)

We reconvened and I filed my findings. Sentences of life without parole were handed down on all murders except the mother-in-law and that sentence was thirty-five years. All sentences were consecutive which meant nothing in this case unless one or more was overturned on appeal.

Two deputies escorted me to my car and I saw and felt the presence of the sister observer. She was headed our way and I suspected that I was about to be cursed and spat upon at the very least. I told the deputies not to interfere with whatever she might do. She was now in my face, raised both arms and hugged my neck while crying on my shoulder. I wept and the deputies wept, but no word was spoken. Closure had come.

The convictions were affirmed on appeal and the forthcoming 3.850 alleging ineffective assistance of counsel was denied and it was affirmed on appeal. I received and filed in the court file a letter from Kingkhamvong Phimmachack. It seemed pointless at the time but looking thru the file to re-fresh my memory for this manuscript I re-read the letter. I perceived that the message was that having judged him I had exposed myself to also being judged. Not someday being judged (my soul)was never considered by me to be an option.

The near awesome powers I exercised in this case and others were, in reality, an absolute burden of heavy responsi-bility. I believe that responsibility, given my experience in jurisprudence, dictates a clear duty to express my present view on the death penalty. My view is that it should be abolished and I realize that my view will draw substantial criticism. But I've been known to wear hair shirts.

During a week in May, 2002 I sat on a First Degree Mur-der case (the death penalty was not sought) and the defendant was acquitted. My daughter Dell had, a day or two later, in-quired about the case and during the conversation I had ex-pressed my present view and was "respectfully" called a "flam-ing liberal." I gave her the following response for my view and she responded, "I will have to seriously think about this":

1) Justice Kogan in a recent article opined that adjudi-cating death penalty issues had seriously hampered the Su-preme Court of Florida in exercising its total jurisdiction;

2) The costs involved for the legal and judicial labor were many times the cost of incarceration for life and the technol-ogy for prevention of escape has improved to the point that escape is really rare;

3) Current events, caused by advances in technology (e.g., DNA), prove that some (too many) innocent are wrong-fully convicted and thus inexcusably sentenced;

4) The ever evolving and narrowing of the cases war-

ranting the death penalty will result in defendants put to death for crimes that would later not result in its application (as I pointed out in this chapter by referring to Spinkelink);

5) And as I pointed out in this chapter, life imprisonment for one with any conscience is worse punishment than death.

Having said that I, with no attempt at modesty, believe that I have the wisdom to determine when the death penalty is warranted (under the law) and would have no qualms in its imposition so long as I was the one imposing the sentence. But even assuming that only I or my true peers would resolve such matters does not solve the problem of John Doe being executed today for a crime that would not warrant Billy Roe's execution ten years hence.

29

A time to fish or cut bait?

The Phimmachak case tried, I returned to Palatka to catch up with my calendar. Whatever anonymity I had was gone. I had already dealt with the life, liberty and property of thousands of fellow Putnam Countians and had been exposed to thousands of jurors. I now had been front page *Palatka Daily News* for several weeks. I avoided, when possible, going into public places because the stares of recognition were ever present and I had no memory of whatever contact the staring people had with the Judge. On many occasions they would want to discuss the matter but they were politely advised that it would be improper.

Effective January 1998 we added a Circuit Judge and were now mandated to have a Family Division. The new Judge was W. A. Parsons and he and his wife Patty lived in Ormond Beach. I suggested to Patty that Miss Sara and I would be pleased to host a "high tea" at the house following the investiture. She accepted knowing that a reception in Ormond would require a one-hour trip from the Courthouse. The high tea was later taken over by Patty and became a catered affair which drew about 300 guests. The house was full but somehow not overcrowded mostly due, I suppose, to the ample pool deck.

Judge Arthur Nichols volunteered to do the first tour in the Family Division and Judge Parsons took over his docket which was fifty percent of everything except family matters. Judge Parsons' practice had been mostly personal injury and insurance and he had very little exposure to criminal justice. He would learn that the criminal docket was never-ending in that for every case disposed of one had been added. He was amazed at the numbers and the atrocities.

I was at First Appearances one Sunday morning and one defendant was charged and arrested for attempted first degree murder. A minor barroom argument had culminated in his raising and thrusting the end of his pool cue into the eye socket of his seated opponent. The eye was pierced to a depth of two and one half inches into the brain. First Appearances are required in Florida for any arrestee who had been in jail for twenty-four hours and not bonded. The primary purpose was to review the reasonableness of the bond which was initially set pursuant to a bond schedule. We rotated this weekend duty among the now four Judges and held them in a small room located in the jail. They usually included twelve to fifteen multi-convicted felons.

This defendant suggested that he needed an unsecured bond which meant that only he would be liable for estreature for non-appearance. He suggested that the incident was an "accident." I suggested that the report indicated that the victim would die within hours and that the death would likely put him in a no-bond status because the case would become capital. The victim died.

I later conducted the trial and the defendant was convicted of murder in the second degree. I sentenced him to the maximum guideline sentence of 35 years in prison. He was in his mid thirties at the time of sentencing and he would be about sixty-five before being released. His abused wife would soon be a regular defendant on my docket.

During post-Phimmachack times I was timing my bar-bershop appearances to the least crowded times in order to avoid the inevitable conversations concerning Phimmachack. Other patrons were surprised that I, seemingly asleep, never joined in and tried not to listen. Leslie thought my haircuts were too short and she arranged (how, I do not know) that Ralph Willis, the owner and operator of the County's most popular hair salon, would do my hair at his home on every third Monday afternoon. Monday was his day off.

I had become St. Mark's Episcopal Church Treasurer in October, 1992 and the church office was across the street from the Willis' home. I would occasionally witness their comings and goings.

Miss Sara and I would occasionally see Ralph and his wife Margaret at social gatherings, but I knew little concern-ing their backgrounds. Ralph soon became the father of Olivia, and I, in turn, became Olivia's "Ganpa". They had started attending our church.

My first haircut at Ralph's home was with some appre-hension because I did not know whether the arrangement was business or social. It was an immediate friendship. Ralph had been in the Marine Corps during the same time we were in Newfoundland. We listened to each other's war stories and slowly fleshed out our backgrounds. The haircuts were only a necessary and minor part of the visits. The conversations were many times led by Ralph into saltwater fishing which he did mostly at Horseshoe Beach on the Gulf of Mexico.

My saltwater fishing experience was very limited. It in-cluded a few trips with Allyson and husband Patrick in the creeks that empty into the Intracoastal Waterway near Cres-cent Beach. They had moved into a home not far from the westerly end of the bridge that was part of SR 206 and spanned the Intracoastal. We had also occasionally surf-fished for whiting. During our almost annual week at a condo in Crescent Beach Stephen and I would be taken fishing by Charlie Baird, a near-by neighbor. Stephen, then about twelve years old, boated a monster saltwater catfish after about a forty-minute struggle. We took it home, took a photograph, and skinned and ate it. During later times we would show the photograph and those in the know swore that it was surely a world record and would have been worth thousands from tackle manufacturers.

Ralph and I made two or three fishing trips to the Intracoastal and did only fair. We made our first overnight trip to Horseshoe and loaded the boat. I was hooked. Horseshoe is located about eighteen miles southwest of Cross City on the Gulf of Mexico, but, in point of time, it was in the 1930's. I had not known that part of the Florida I grew up in still existed. I had the fever and that would require a boat. I ultimately wound up with a twenty-two foot pontoon boat set up for very comfortable fishing.

The haircutting and fishing produced one of my closest friends. The addition of the new Judge meant splitting the total caseload three ways instead of two. It was like the move to Moody AFB in that I went from being overworked to being underworked. Obsessive/compulsives don't thrive on being underworked but it now meant that I could take my allotted vacation, whereas before, taking the allotted time meant doing the same workload in a compressed time period.

During 1998 I started calendaring as many Mondays as possible to "sit" in the Gulf of Mexico with Ralph. We left after the 8 a.m. Sunday Eucharist and were on the water by about 1 p.m. We fished that afternoon and the next day, leaving the water at about 3:30 pm. We caught fish, fish and more fish and began to have a waiting list of possible guests. Curtis Horton, a retired flower grower, was one such guest and after his trip he later allowed to Ralph that he had never seen a fisherman who fished harder than the Judge. He had observed my tantrum at losing (broken line) a thirty-two inch gator trout. He wondered how judges became acquainted with such language. Miss Sara allowed that she would soon buy us left- and right-handed reels which would make fishing easier since Ralph and I had become "joined at the hip".

During these trips I began to reflect on retirement. All I was experiencing was a repetition of cases I had handled hundreds of times before. Time and gravity had recently added a tummy boot for a hernia. I began to understand Miss Kate's concern with not "staying past your time" and my time included almost forty years in criminal justice systems. Things I saw and routinely heard daily would put most "normal" people in shock. I had seen it on the faces of jurors. I often amused others by stating that I was "warped or at least entitled to be warped".

In January 2001 I would have to begin my eighteen month tour in the Family Division doing only juvenile and domestic relations. These were the most stressful of all cases and I sometimes felt guilt for the near-perfectness of our family life. We had put four children through college and they were all happily married and self-supporting. The fall of 2000 seemed the perfect time to retire but, for a Citra boy, it seemed that I would be "quitting" my job for no good reason.

Part of the problem was I had to admit that I was obsessive/compulsive even in fishing. (My wife often opined that I was obsessive/compulsive and anal retentive.) Obsessive/compulsives having been where the rubber met the road for forty years simply could not tolerate doing nothing. One retired Judge put it this way: "When you're doing nothing, it's hard to tell when you're finished". I considered cattle-raising but that would require an employee during hoped-for trips to spend time with the other twin. I didn't want any more employees. I considered some more cabin building in Hiawassee but I knew that Miss Sara's separation from her then eight grandchildren would only be for short periods. Maybe I could enter the building business with SLB, Jr and drive him crazy. In September, 1999 I thought I had substantially completed this manuscript in less than two months. My editor, Jim Mast, opined that I had barely begun and he was right. Maybe I would do all of the above and write in my spare time. I also wondered that I was fretting since the right choices in my life had a habit of presenting themselves at the right time.

One retirement was not an apparent option and that was as Church Treasurer. The Rev. Canon Robert F. Marsh, Jr. had become Parish Priest in 1992 and soon nominated me to the Vestry to serve as Church Treasurer. He had jokingly promised that he would teach me everything I never wanted to know about church finances. I had overseen budgets as Staff Judge Advocate, State Attorney, and Chief Administrative Judge for Putnam County. The day-to-day transactions and reports of such matters were handled by the "bean counters" and they had many quirks which usually included why I was spending "their" money. Pride and a haughty spirit had caught up with me again. I had become a bean counter without benefit of an accounting degree.

Musing aloud with Fr. Bob one day, now a close friend and sometimes fishing partner, I asked his view on my retirement. He said, "You mean as Treasurer or Judge?" I started to say "Both," but he explained that one Treasurer had served thirty-seven years and died in office. I could see in his eyes

that he knew my obsessive/compulsive nature would require an effort to outdo such a predecessor. Such an effort could be completed by the time I was about ninety-five years of age.

30

The death of the Queen Mother

In mid-year 1999 Miss Florence's health began to fail. She was ninety-four and the body organs were simply wearing out.

We consulted with our family physician, Dr. John Collette, who lived and practiced in Crescent City but also did house calls. John Collette (also a family friend) was no less than a genius in family health care but unlike many his genius was paired with street smarts. Pair that with his humane goodness and you had the perfect doctor/person to minister to Miss Florence during her "last" days (she knew it to be so).

The proper pairing of doctor and patient was amply demonstrated by the last visit Miss Florence had with a young female doctor in Gainesville. That doctor had suggested the visit would include a complete physical which, in turn, would include intrusion into several body cavities. Miss Florence's reaction was, ". . . Not now, not ever, Honey. . ." This lady's life and times were near the top even in the greatest generation and included the adoption of three children when adoption was not all that popular.

On the first visit Dr. John explained our options:

1) We could keep her home but only in the main downstairs of the house (to avoid the steps in her antique shop) and he could keep her comfortable mainly by preventing fluid

build-up caused by the weak heart or

2) We could do the hospital thing which would require diagnostic procedures involving many tubes and needles. He explained that she would not always be lucid and that we should therefore discuss it with her and let him know.

Finally he advised that we, with his help, could keep her out of a nursing home and added that you could never defeat Mother Nature.

We consulted with Miss Florence, our children and Miss Sara's sister and brother and a consensus was easily reached: we would comfort and succor and let her die the dignified death she so richly deserved.

It worked well notwithstanding that Miss Sara was still keeping several grandchildren toddlers (and babies) during the work week. Miss Nancy (Miss Sara's sister) was often there and I did relief shifts but the real burden (and I hesitate to describe it as such because it really blessed all our lives) was on Miss Sara.

We moved our "Lincoln Bed" downstairs and into the living room. Miss Florence had her privacy when she wanted it but more often than not she was with her great grandchildren in the family room. Early on she would frequently express a desire to go "home". I finally lucked onto a response that worked. ". . . Miss Florence you are home, you are the Queen Mother and as such this is your home and your presence graces us all. . ."

A routine rapidly developed and, early on, she was lucid most of the time and thoroughly enjoyed the Queen Mother thing (actually an apt description). The routine was my relieving Miss Sara during the weekends in order that she could do her shopping and have time to herself. We placed a monitor near the family room recliner and when Miss Sara needed a night off for bridge my tour began. I "dozed" in the chair. During the weekend days my time with her was usually spent on the screen porch, bird and squirrel watching. She had a favorite wrought iron (antique of course) rocking chair and I heard the entire story of her life — during bridge nights I also heard the story of Miss Sara's life and was often told, ". . .Lewis you have been so good to me and I am so very, very grateful. . ."

Dr. John attended to her every Sunday and did examinations which did not include intrusions. She was slowly deteriorating but still had many lucid and comfortable times. Early one morning (about 5 a.m.) I had heard nothing on the monitor and I checked. She was dressed and seated in the dining room and inquired, ". . . Lewis, would you make me some coffee. . .". Miss Sara discovered us a couple of hours later and was slightly dismayed that this pair had been chatting about the good old days in Newfoundland.

Slowly, assisting in bathing and bathroom habits, the "burden" was shifted more and more to Miss Sara and I marveled at the quality of this tender loving care. I was also in awe observing the perfect daughter (because of her congestive heart condition I knew that she had begun to draw down reserve strength). I strangely (maybe not) concluded that if my observations could be filmed and shown to the world humanity would be substantially enhanced.

On December 18, 1999 (one day shy of our actual fortieth wedding anniversary) our children hosted (at our home) a wedding anniversary party. Three hundred or so family and friends helped us celebrate and it was a joyous and outstanding affair. Miss Florence almost stole our place in the spotlight. During cake cutting time in the dining room she was center piece and when I introduced her as the Queen Mother she was beaming and basking. She was totally lucid, animated and happy.

Following the party she rapidly deteriorated. Early in January, 2000 we rented a hospital bed because of fear that she would fall and break a hip. On January 7, 2000 while Miss Nancy was relieving Miss Sara she peacefully left this world quietly exclaiming "Yes, yes" in a tone that surely meant she was happily meeting her maker. Miss Sara in particular and the family in general were serene and content that the right thing had been done.

31

'Retirement' and fishing or cutting bait

December 30, 1999 was my 65th birthday and I had been in the work force about fifty-seven years. Following Miss Kate's lead, I decided it was time to consider whether I would be "past my time" before my present term ended. I had about three years to go.

I carefully catalogued the factors for and against retirement and assigned a weight to each. The factors for retirement were: sitting four or five days as a Senior Judge my retirement income would not be materially less than my judicial salary; I would have more time on the boat cutting bait for the children, grandchildren and Ralph; Miss Sara and I could get out of the heat by spending summers in Maine; I could wake up with every day being a Saturday instead of a Monday; I would be able to assist Miss Sara in her home day care center for grandchildren; there would be more time for Church Treasurer duties and I would simply have more time to do what I wanted to do. Against retirement the factors were: a nagging suspicion that I was "quitting" a good job; that the chance of ever attaining any status akin to the "greatest generation" would be over; and if I stayed for the term my judicial retirement pay would be higher.

It was a tough decision. Only the thought of entering the full time Family Division in the upcoming January overrode the quite weighty "quitting my job". As son, brother, nephew, grandson, husband, father and grandfather I had been blessed far beyond my worth. That would make me feel "guilty" while adjudicating the issues involved in the family division and that would not be healthy for my psyche; and that, in turn, would not be healthy for my family relationships. Miss Sara had unintentionally exacerbated this guilt by stating,"...You know, with your life, family and legal experiences you are exceptionally qualified to render true justice in such matters. . ."

I set my retirement for September 30, 2000 and by using vacation time my last work day would be September 14. That afternoon was criminal sentencings. I still dreaded the last day and conjured up in my mind that it would be similar to Shane, in the movie "Shane," riding off into the night after shooting all the bad guys. Joey was following while exclaiming over and over, "Shane, come back! Shane, we don't want you to go!" My scenario would be to sentence all the bad guys to prison, mount my pickup truck and ride off into the night while the Courthouse gang shouted, "Come back Judge Louie, we don't want you to go!" Somehow I believed that I would then regain my anonymity and privacy.

My announced retirement had produced an interview with Mark Lane, a reporter with the *Daytona News Journal.* He was an old friend and he did a splendid feature story highly complimentary of my career and family. Bill Townsend had then called and indicated it was my "duty" to let the Putnam Bar celebrate my last day with a roast. It drew a crowd and it was a fierce roast but it was also a true tribute to my public service. It was an affair that I and my family thoroughly enjoyed and will cherish forever. I was told that most of the crowd teared when I gave Miss Sara credit for all our successes.

The following Monday, purposefully putting off that Monday when I would wake up with nothing to do and nowhere to go, Miss Sara and I boarded Amtrak and rolled to Boston. We rented a car and drove (partially ferried) to Newfoundland. We explored the entire western half of the island and I took a side trip to the radar site which included the lake I never landed on. It was a wonderful vacation and Newfoundland was more remote, barren and rugged than I remembered. That for me is still its beauty. On my suggestion that we should often return to Newfoundland Miss Sara had replied, ". . .I agree, we can go back every forty years. . ."

My guilt for quitting was rapidly erased. As Senior Judge I "was being recalled to active duty" about eight or ten days per month to try/resolve difficult cases that had exasperated the assigned judges. One such case was seven years old and had not been resolved by five different judges. My persistence resolved it. It is a perfect "retirement". I mused that I would be age ninety-five before I attained sufficient faith not to fret.

During one of those assignments one of my best Assistant State Attorneys tracked me down in the hallway of the Volusia County Justice Center. Among other things he told me ". . .you have always been my role model as a lawyer. . ." and also indicated that I had been like a father to him. The war orphan had to fight tearing up (not totally successfully). He said that it needed to be said.

It has been a long road but it seems that it should have taken more time to travel. It has been a great personal life because of the love of my family and many true friends. As a son of the "Greatest Generation" I could have done no less than be a man of principle. The high standards of those who have gone before me, while sometimes seeming a burden, have sustained me in making stressful decisions. I believe my children and their children and the descendants yet to come will read these reminiscences and believe that I was, at least most of the time, trying to follow in the path made by great shoes.

Finally, my professional caseload was so heavy that I doubtless made mistakes. But the mistakes were made by the mind and not the heart. As the Phimmachak lawyers believed, no decision I ever made was infected with fear, favor or hope of reward.